THE BIG BOOK OF BBQ SAUCES

212 Barbecue Sauces Straight from the Pitmaster

Frank Mueller

About the Author____ **170**

BARBECUE SAUCES

HOW TO BUILD AN AWESOME BBQ SAUCE

When it comes to BBQ sauces, the only rule is that there is no rule. The ingredients of these sauces can range from coffee to cough syrup. As long as the portions and proportions are balanced, the possibilities of ingredients that can be thrown into a BBQ sauce are limited only by your imagination. However, when making your own barbecue cause, always try to combine contrasting elements—sweet, sour, salty, aromatic, hot—into a wholesome blend.

Here's a look at the indispensable building blocks you need to make a great barbecue sauce.

THE BASE

The base is... well... the base, the foundation of a BBQ sauce. A few popular bases for barbecue sauce include:

- Chicken or beef stock
- Chili sauce
- Fresh tomatoes
- Ketchup
- Mayonnaise
- Mustard
- Tomato sauce/tomato purée/tomato paste

- Vinegar

THE SWEETENERS

Most BBQ sauces contain a sweetening element. A few of the most popular sweeteners are:

- **Cane syrup:** Sweet with a rich mouthfeel.
- **Corn syrup (light or dark):** Less sweet than cane sugar, with a rich mouthfeel.
- **Granulated sugar:** The common white sugar you use to sweeten your coffee.
- **Honey:** Sweet with a floral flavour.
- **Jams and jellies:** Sweet, fruity flavour.
- **Light or dark brown sugar:** Sweet with a molasses flavour.
- **Maple sugar/maple syrup:** Less sweet than cane sugar, with a musky maple flavour.
- **Molasses:** Sweet and earthy.
- **Piloncillo:** Unrefined Mexican brown sugar. Sweet with an earthy, malty molasses flavour.
- **Rice syrup:** Sold in natural foods stores. Less sweet than cane sugar, with earthy malt flavours.
- **Sucanat:** Freeze-dried sugarcane juice; sold in natural foods stores. Sweet with a malty flavour.

- **Turbinado sugar (Sugar in the Raw brand):** A granulated light brown sugar that gets its color from an added trace of molasses.

THE SOURING AGENTS

All popular BBQ sauces out there contain at least one souring agent. A few of the most commonly used ones are:

- **Balsamic vinegar:** Acidic with a fruity sweetness.
- **Cider vinegar:** Acidic with a fruity finish.
- **Distilled vinegar:** Just plain sour.
- **Lemon juice:** Tart with a fruity flavour; occasionally whole lemons are added to a sauce, adding a bitter element as well as acidic.
- **Lime juice and sour orange juice:** Work in the same way as lemon juice.
- **Pickle juice:** Yum!
- **Tamarind:** Sour-sweet smoky flavour.
- **Wine vinegar:** Acidic with a wine flavour.

THE SEASONINGS

No sauce is complete without seasoning. Here are the most commonly used ones:

- **Anchovy fillets/paste:** An ingredient in many steak sauces.

- **Capers:** The pickled buds of a Mediterranean flowering shrub; salty and tangy.
- **Fish sauce:** Salt with a Southeast Asian accent.
- **Hoisin sauce:** A thick Chinese condiment that's both salty and sweet.
- **Miso:** Cultured soybean paste; available in many colors and flavours. Salt with a luscious umami finish.
- **Olives:** Especially salty olives, like Kalamata or Sicilian.
- **Salt:** In particular, sea salt or kosher salt
- **Soy sauce:** Salt with an Asian accent.
- **Sun-dried tomatoes:** Dried or oil-packed, your choice.

THE HEAT

The signature element of sauces from Texas, South-West America, etc. Here are a few of the most common ingredients:

- **Black and white pepper:** Grind it fresh for extra flavour.
- **Fresh chile peppers:** Pretty much every variety can be used.
- **Fresh ginger:** Minced or grated.
- **Ground cayenne pepper and red pepper flakes: These impart heat gradually.**
- **Horseradish:** Best used fresh or added at the last minute, as the heat depletes with time.
- **Hot sauce:** Tabasco, Crystal Hot Sauce, Texas Pete, Cholula, etc are a few of the popular ones.

- **Mustard:** Both prepared and powdered forms are used.
- <u>Wasabi</u>: An insanely delicious Japanese condiment, similar in properties to horseradish.

THE AROMATICS

Aromatics are strong flavouring agents, so make sure you don't use them in excess. Here are a few of the common ingredients in BBQ sauces:

- **Bell peppers and poblano chiles: Nutritious and Flavourful. Use fresh.**
- **Celery:** Celery seed and celery salt, best used fresh.
- **Chili powder:** Essential for Texas BBQ Sauces.
- **Garlic:** Used fresh, dried, powdered, or in garlic salt form.
- **Herbs:** Basil, bay leaf, chives, cilantro, dill, marjoram, mint, oregano, parsley, rosemary, thyme, etc. are a few of the common herbs used in BBQ sauces.
- **Liquid smoke:** Imparts the flavour of wood smoke to the sauce.
- **Onions:** Can be used fresh, dried, powdered, or in onion salt form.
- **Spices:** The list is endless. All kinds of spices with all kinds of flavours are used in BBQ sauces.
- **Steak sauce:** Tastes like salted tomatoes, with a hint of raisin and orange.
- **Worcestershire sauce:** Sweet, salty, and aromatic!

ENRICHERS

These greatly enhance the texture of the sauce, making it look absolutely spectacular!

- **Bacon/bacon fat:** Imparts a rich smoky flavour.
- **Beef stock/chicken stock:** Imparts a rich meaty flavour without fat.
- **Butter:** Salted or unsalted.
- **Lard:** Classic fat used for frying Mexican salsas.
- **Meat drippings:** The secret ingredient in many BBQ sauces.
- **Oil:** Olive, sesame, walnut, and hazelnut impart flavour as well as richness; vegetable oil is merely rich.

RANDOM STUFF

Random unexpected ingredients sometimes go great in BBQ sauces. A few of these ingredients are:

- **Coffee:** Adds an extra boost of energy and flavour to BBQ sauces.
- **Peanut butter:** A common ingredient in sauces of Thailand and Indonesia.
- **Soda:** Cola, root beer, ginger ale, lemon-lime, and orange soda, etc. sometimes go great in BBQ sauces!
- **Spirits:** Bourbon, rye, Scotch, brandy, rum, and tequila can be great additions to BBQ sauces!

- **Vanilla extract:** Imparts a familiar sweetness.
- **Water:** if the sauce tastes too strong, add water to it!
- **Wine:** Great for adding some much-needed acidity.

BASIC DIRECTIONS

Every recipe in this book has individual directions, but the rules are generally the same. If you're looking to invent a BBQ sauce of your own, or tweaking a recipe already in this book, here are the directions you will usually need to follow:

1. Simply throw the ingredients into a pot and bring to a boil.
2. Next, decrease the heat and simmer, stirring barely enough to stop it from burning.

Some complex recipes might have a few additional steps, but this is the gist of it. Time to jump into the recipes!

BASIC BARBEQUE SAUCE

Homemade barbecue sauce is always better than a store-bought one!

Ingredients:

- ½ cup cider vinegar
- ½ teaspoon liquid smoke
- 1 cup ketchup
- 1 cup tomato sauce
- 1 cup water
- 1 green bell pepper, finely chopped
- 1 onion, finely chopped
- 1 tablespoon Worcestershire sauce
- 1 teaspoon cayenne pepper
- 1 teaspoon dry mustard
- 2 tablespoons lemon juice
- 2 tablespoons molasses
- 3 tablespoons vegetable oil

Directions:

1. In a big deep cooking pan, heat oil and sauté the onion and bell pepper for approximately 3 to five minutes using medium heat.

2. Put in the rest of the ingredients and simmer using low heat for an hour. Store in an airtight jar in the refrigerator for maximum 2 weeks.

Yield: 3 cups

AIOLI

A garlic-flavoured homemade mayonnaise from Provence. Serve with grilled vegetables and meats.

Ingredients:

- ¼ teaspoon freshly ground black pepper
- ¼ teaspoon sea salt
- 1½ cups extra-virgin olive oil
- 4 fresh organic egg yolks
- 4 to 6 cloves garlic, minced

Directions:

1. Use a food processor to mix egg yolks, garlic, salt, and pepper. Slowly put in olive oil to blend.
2. Store in your fridge for maximum 3 days.

Yield: 1¾ cups

ALABAMA WHITE SAUCE

Goes great with chicken and fish!

Ingredients:

- ¼ teaspoon ground red pepper
- ½ teaspoon salt
- 1 cup cider vinegar
- 1 cup mayonnaise
- 1 tablespoon lemon juice
- 1½ tablespoons cracked black pepper

Directions:

1. Mix all of the ingredients in a big glass jar with a tight-fitting lid.
2. Close the lid and shake to combine. Store in your fridge for quite a few weeks.

Yield: 2 cups

ALL PURPOSE SAUCE

Ingredients:

- ¼ cup bourbon
- ¼ cup salad oil
- ½ tsp. black pepper
- 1 tsp. garlic powder
- 1 tsp. Worcestershire sauce

- 2 tbs. soy sauce

Directions:

1. Enjoy Raw!
2. Blend ingredients and pour over any meat or fish as a marinade or use as a baste.

APPLE AND MINT SAUCE

Time Taken: 5 minutes

Ingredients:

- ¼ teaspoon salt
- ½ cup white rice vinegar
- 1 cup apple, chunks
- 1 teaspoon garlic paste
- 1 teaspoons white pepper
- 2 tablespoons mint leaves

Directions:

1. Move all ingredients into food processor and pulse well.
2. Put in to container and use with chicken, pork or steaks.
3. Enjoy.

APPLE-BACON BUTTER

Serve as a side condiment with beef or game.

Ingredients:

- ½ cup (1 stick) butter softened
- 1 tablespoon chopped chives
- 1 tablespoon minced onion
- 1 teaspoon Worcestershire sauce
- 2 slices apple-bacon, cooked crisp
- 2 tablespoons crumbled Roquefort cheese

Directions:

1. Mix butter, Roquefort, and Worcestershire sauce and cream until fluffy.
2. Put in bacon, onion, and chives and place in your fridge to chill.

Yield: ¾ cup

APRICOT GLAZE FOR HAM

Ingredients:

- 1 tablespoon ground cloves
- 1½ tablespoons cider vinegar
- 2 cups apricot preserves
- 2½ teaspoons dry mustard

Directions:

Mix all of the ingredients and coat ham.

Yield: 2 cups

APRICOT-PLUM SAUCE

Best served with chicken, turkey, quail, or other game recipes.

Ingredients:

- ½ cup apricot preserves
- 1 cup plum jelly or jam
- 1 teaspoon sugar
- 1 teaspoon white vinegar

Directions:

1. Mix all of the ingredients in a blender or food processor.
2. Cover and place in your fridge until ready to use. Store in an airtight jar in your fridge for maximum several weeks.

Yield: 1½ cups

AROMATIC CASSEROLE SAUCE

Ingredients:

- ¼ cup salad oil

- ¼ tsp. Paprika
- ½ cup catsup
- ½ tsp. garlic powder
- ½ tsp. mustard powder
- ½ tsp. Salt
- 1 tsp. grated onion
- 1 tsp. Worcestershire sauce
- 1/3 cup white vinegar
- 1/8 tsp. hot sauce

Directions:

1. Put ingredients in container and mix thoroughly.
2. Pour a small amount n a casserole dish a coat bottom of dish.
3. Put 3 pounds of cut up chicken or meat in casserole and pour remaining sauce on op.
4. Bake using your oven, turning a couple of times, until done.

BASTING SAUCE FOR POULTRY OR PORK

Can also be used as a marinade.

Ingredients:

- ⅓ cup vinegar
- ½ cup olive oil
- 1 teaspoon freshly grated ginger
- 1 teaspoon ground coriander
- 1 teaspoon ground cumin
- 2 cloves garlic, minced
- 2 tablespoons honey
- 2 tablespoons lemon juice
- 2 tablespoons Worcestershire sauce

Directions:

1. Put all of the ingredients in a big glass jar with a tight-fitting lid. Shake to combine.
2. Store in your fridge for maximum 1 month.

Yield: 1⅓ cups

BBQ CIDER SAUCE

Ingredients:

- ¼ cup salt
- ¼ tsp. liquid smoke
- ½ cup ginger ale
- ¾ tbs. cayenne pepper
- 1 qt apple cider vinegar
- 1 tbs. brown sugar

- 1 tbs. red pepper flakes

Directions:

1. Mix vinegar and salt in a deep cooking pan and bring to its boiling point.
2. Turn off the heat and put in remaining ingredients.
3. Stir until thoroughly combined.

BBQ SWEET SAUCE

Ingredients:

- ¼ tsp. rosemary
- ½ cup red wine vinegar
- ½ tsp. black pepper
- 1 bottle chili sauce (14 ounces)
- 1 can applesauce
- 1 clove garlic, mashed
- 1 tbs. Worcestershire sauce
- 1 tsp. salt

Directions:

1. Mix ingredients in a glass container and mix thoroughly.
2. Cover and allow it to stand for about two hours before you use.

BEACH VINEGAR SAUCE

Goes great on grilled seafood and poultry!

Ingredients:

- ¼ cup dark rum
- ½ cup dark brown sugar
- ½ cup freshly squeezed orange juice
- 1 cup rice wine vinegar
- 1 tablespoon freshly grated ginger
- 2 tablespoons lime juice
- 2 tablespoons Thai chili sauce
- 2 teaspoons dry mustard
- Zest from 1 lime

Directions:

1. In a big deep cooking pan, reduce rum by half on moderate to high heat.
2. Put in the rest of the ingredients and cook on moderate to low heat for 20 to half an hour. Store in an airtight jar in the refrigerator for maximum 2 weeks.

Yield: 2 cups

BÉARNAISE SAUCE

Béarnaise is conventionally served with meat, fish, eggs, or vegetables.

Ingredients:

- ¼ cup dry white wine
- ¼ cup tarragon vinegar
- ¼ teaspoon salt
- ¼ teaspoon Tabasco
- ½ cup (1 stick) unsalted butter
- ½ tablespoon chopped fresh parsley
- 1 tablespoon chopped fresh tarragon
- 2 tablespoons hot water
- 3 egg yolks

Directions:

1. In a twofold boiler, melt butter slowly using moderate heat.
2. Whisk in hot water and remove top of twofold boiler from the heat to cool.
3. Put top of twofold boiler back on pot. Whisk in egg yolks and then the rest of the ingredients. Over low heat, stir continuously until thick.

Yield: 1½ cups

BEEF BRUSH SAUCE

Ingredients:

- ¼ cup red wine vinegar
- ½ cup salad oil
- 1 clove garlic, crushed
- 1 cup water
- 1 tbs. black pepper
- 1 tbs. brown sugar
- 1 tbs. dry mustard
- 1 tbs. paprika
- 1 tbs. Salt
- 1 tsp. Italian seasoning
- 2 tbs. chili sauce
- 2 tbs. ground horseradish
- 2 tbs. onion, grated
- 2 tbs. Worcestershire sauce

Directions:

1. Put ingredients in a deep cooking pan and simmer for fifteen minutes, stirring once in a while.

BIG MIX BBQ SAUCE

Ingredients:

- 1 big onion, minced
- 1 tsp. ground red pepper

- 1 tsp. MSG
- 3 bay leaves, crumbled
- 3 cups dark brown sugar, packed
- 3 tbs. Panola sauce
- 3 tbs. Pickapeppa sauce
- 3 tsp. Tabasco
- 4 cups water
- 4 tbs. corn starch (for thickening)
- 6 ¼ tsp. mustard powder
- 6 tbs. black pepper
- 6 tbs. chili powder
- 6 tbs. salt
- 6 tbs. sugar
- 7 cups white vinegar
- 9 cups catsup

Directions:

1. Combine all ingredientsin a big vat and bring to a rolling boil.
2. Decrease the heat to low and simmer for 5 hours. Stir frequently.
3. Eat immediately or bottle and cure.
4. Cure for approximately one week.

BLUE CHEESE SAUCE

This sauce tastes insane with poultry or grilled or raw vegetables.

Ingredients:

- ¼ teaspoon seasoned pepper
- ½ cup light mayonnaise
- ½ cup light sour cream
- ½ teaspoon Tabasco sauce
- 4 ounces blue cheese, crumbled

Directions:

1. Mix all of the ingredients in a blender or food processor. Blend until the desired smoothness is achieved.
2. Store in your fridge for maximum one week.

Yield: 1 cup

BLUEBERRY CITRUS SAUCE

Goes great with grilled veal, game, and poultry.

Ingredients:

- 1 cup blueberries, fresh or frozen
- 1 tablespoon fresh minced ginger
- 2 tablespoons grated lemon peel
- 2 tablespoons grated orange peel
- 2 tablespoons lemon juice

- 2 tablespoons sugar
- 2 tablespoons vermouth

Directions:

1. In a small deep cooking pan, mix all of the ingredients. Bring to its boiling point on moderate to high heat.
2. Blueberries will start to pop open and mixture will thicken. Turn off the heat and serve warm, or place in your fridge and serve cold.
3. Store in the refrigerator for maximum one week.

Yield: 1¼ cups

BORDER BBQ SAUCE

Goes great with shrimp, chicken, beef, and pork.

Ingredients:

- ½ bunch fresh cilantro, chopped
- ½ cup spicy tomato barbecue sauce
- 2 teaspoons fresh lime juice

Directions:

1. Mix all of the ingredients in a glass container and serve as a dipping sauce.
2. Use instantly.

Yield: 1 cup

BOURBON BBQ SAUCE

Try this sauce on slow-smoked brisket and spareribs.

Ingredients:

- ¼ cup bourbon
- ¼ cup cider vinegar
- ½ cup orange marmalade
- 1 cup chili sauce
- 1 cup ketchup
- 1 small onion, chopped
- 1 tablespoon olive oil
- 1 tablespoon Tabasco sauce
- 1 teaspoon ground pepper
- 2 tablespoons Dijon mustard
- 2 teaspoons Worcestershire sauce

Directions:

1. Sauté onion in oil in a big deep cooking pan using medium heat. Put in the rest of the ingredients and bring to its boiling point.
2. Reduce heat and simmer for about half an hour, stirring frequently until it becomes thick.

Yield: 3 cups

BROWN SUGAR AND TOMATO SAUCE

Time Taken: ten minutes

Ingredients:

- ½ cup brown sugar
- ½ teaspoon chili powder
- 1 teaspoon ginger powder
- 2 cup tomato puree
- 2 garlic cloves minced
- 3 tablespoons red wine vinegar

Directions:

1. In a deep cooking pan put in tomato puree and cook for five minutes on low heat.
2. Now put in vinegar, sugar, chili powder, garlic, ginger, and stir.
3. Turn off heat and move into a container.
4. Use grilled chicken or steaks.

CALIFORNIA-STYLE BARBECUE SAUCE

Ingredients:

- ¼ cup balsamic vinegar
- ¼ cup Worcestershire sauce
- ½ cup dark honey

- 1 big white onion, finely chopped
- 1 cup chili sauce
- 1 Knorr beef bouillon cube
- 1 teaspoon chopped fresh oregano
- 1 teaspoon chopped fresh thyme
- 2 cloves garlic, minced
- 2 tablespoons extra virgin olive oil
- 2 tablespoons soy sauce
- 2 teaspoons wasabi powder or paste
- Sea salt and freshly ground black pepper to taste

Directions:

1. In a big frying pan, heat olive oil and sauté onion and garlic until translucent.
2. Mix in the rest of the ingredients and simmer for half an hour. Store in an airtight jar in your fridge for maximum 3 weeks.

Yield: 3 cups

CARPACCIO SAUCE

A yummy sauce that goes great with grilled meats and seafood like beef tenderloin and tuna steaks.

Ingredients:

- ¼ cup capers

- ¼ cup white wine vinegar
- ⅓ cup Dijon mustard
- ¾ cup olive oil
- 12 gherkins
- 2 cloves garlic, minced
- 2 cups packed fresh parsley
- 2 tablespoons capers for decoration
- 3 anchovy fillets
- 3 tablespoons chopped onion

Directions:

1. Use a food processor to mix parsley, ¼ cup capers, gherkins, anchovies, garlic, onion, vinegar, and mustard.
2. Slowly put in olive oil in a thin stream to blend. Remove from processor and mix in the rest of the 2 tablespoons capers. Serve instantly.

Yield: 1½ cups

CAVIAR MAYONNAISE

For a festive occasion, serve this decadent sauce with a platter of grilled or steamed vegetables.

Ingredients:

- ½ cup mayonnaise
- 2 tablespoons lemon juice

- 2 tablespoons salmon caviar

Directions:

1. Mix mayonnaise and lemon juice, then gently mix in caviar.
2. Place in your fridge to chill. Serve with grilled lobster tails.

Yield: ¾ cup

CELERY BBQ SAUCE

Ingredients:

- ½ cup lemon juice
- ½ tsp. hot sauce
- 1 bottle catsup (24 ounce)
- 1 cup brown sugar
- 1 small onion, minced
- 1 tbs. celery seed
- 1 tsp. black pepper
- 1 tsp. liquid smoke
- 1 tsp. Salt
- 2 cloves garlic, minced
- 2 cups vinegar
- 2 tbs. butter or margarine
- 2 tbs. Worcestershire sauce
- 3 stalks celery, chopped fine

Directions:

1. Melt butter in a deep cooking pan and sauté onions, garlic and celery until soft.
2. Put in rest of the ingredients and simmer on moderate heat for fifteen minutes, stirring once in a while.

CHILI AND HONEY MUSTARD SAUCE

Time Taken: 5 minutes

Ingredients:

- ½ cup chili sauce
- ½ cup honey
- 1 teaspoon garlic powder
- 2 tablespoons mustard powder
- 2 tablespoons soya sauce

Directions:

1. Take a container and put in chili sauce, soya sauce, honey, mustard powder, garlic powder and stir until blended well.
2. Serve with your salad.

CHILI-HOISIN SAUCE

Ingredients:

- ¼ cup dark brown sugar, packed
- ½ cup Hoisin sauce
- ½ tsp. ground ginger
- 1 cup chili sauce

Directions:

1. Put ingredients in a deep cooking pan and stir using low heat, until sugar melts and mixture is smooth.

CHILLI KAHLUA SAUCE

Ingredients:

- ½ cup chili sauce
- ¾ cup Kahlua
- 2 tbs. cornstarch
- 3 tbs. pineapple juice

Directions:

1. Mix first 3 ingredients in a deep cooking pan using low heat.
2. Make smooth, thin paste with cornstarch and water.
3. Mix in paste slowly.
4. Simmer for fifteen minutes or until sauce begins to thicken.

CHILLI ZESTY CATSUP BBQ SAUCE

Ingredients:

- ¼ cup brown sugar
- ¼ cup onion, chopped fine
- ¼ cup salad oil
- ¼ cup water
- ½ cup Worcestershire sauce
- 1 ¼ cup catsup
- 1 beef bouillon cube
- 1 tbs. hot pepper sauce
- 1/3 cup lemon juice

Directions:

1. Mix ingredients in deep cooking pan and cook using low heat
2. for approximately one hour, stirring once in a while.
3. Cook until sauce becomes thick.
4. Serve warm.

CHIMICHURRI SAUCE-MARINADE

This Argentinian steak sauce is conventionally served with pit-smoked beef.

Ingredients:

- ¼ cup red wine vinegar
- ½ cup olive oil
- 1 teaspoon dried oregano
- 1 teaspoon red pepper flakes
- 2 teaspoons chopped fresh parsley
- 4 cloves garlic, chopped
- Salt and freshly ground black pepper to taste

Directions:

1. Mix all of the ingredients in a jar with lid.
2. Let sit at room temperature for 1 day, or warm to approximately 120 degrees F for one to two minutes, then let it stand for an hour to combine.
3. Put meat and marinade using plastic bag for an hour before grilling. Store in an airtight jar in the refrigerator for maximum 2 weeks.

Yield: ⅔ cup

CHINESE BBQ SAUCE

Ingredients:

- ½ cup Hoisin sauce
- ½ cup soy sauce
- 1 chicken bouillon cube
- 3 tbs. honey

- 3 tbs. salad oil
- 3 tbs. Sherry
- 3 tbs. sugar
- 3 tbs. water
- 4 cloves garlic, minced

Directions:

1. Mix ingredients in a deep cooking pan, stirring continuously, using low heat.
2. Stir until super smooth.

CHIVE-SHALLOT VINAIGRETTE

Serve this warm vinaigrette sprinkled over a grilled shellfish or seafood salad. It is also a great basting mixture for meats and vegetables.

Ingredients:

- 1 tablespoon lemon juice
- 1 tablespoon snipped Italian parsley
- 2 tablespoons snipped chives
- 3 cloves garlic, minced
- 4 shallots, finely chopped
- 4 tablespoons butter
- 4 tablespoons white wine vinegar

½ cup olive oil

Directions:

1. Sauté shallots and garlic in butter on moderate to low heat until tender for about five minutes.
2. Put in vinegar, lemon juice, chives, and parsley and sauté for a couple of minutes more. Whisk in olive oil, then turn off the heat. Store in an airtight jar in your fridge for maximum 5 days.

Yield: 1¼ cups

CHUCKWAGON SAUCE

Ingredients:

- ½ cup butter or margarine
- ½ cup salad oil
- 1 big onion, grated
- 1 can tomato sauce
- 1 cup black coffee
- 1 cup white vinegar
- 1 cup Worcestershire sauce
- 1 tbs. salt
- 1 tbs. sugar
- 1 tsp. hot sauce
- 2 tsp. black pepper
- 2 tsp. chili powder

Directions:

1. Put ingredients in a deep cooking pan and bring to its boiling point.
2. Decrease the heat and simmer, uncovered, for fifteen minutes.
3. Stir once in a while.

CHUNKY WESTERN SAUCE

Ingredients:

- ¼ cup red wine vinegar
- ¼ tsp. cayenne pepper
- ¼ tsp. hot sauce
- ½ cup catsup
- ½ pound butter or margarine
- 1 big onion, chopped
- 1 can tomato paste
- 1 can tomatoes
- 1 clove garlic, minced
- 2 bay leaves, crushed
- 2 cups water
- 2 tbs. lemon juice
- 2 tbs. sugar
- 2 tsp. black pepper
- 2 tsp. dry mustard

- 2 tsp. Worcestershire sauce
- 3 tsp. chili powder

Directions:

1. Mix ingredients in deep cooking pan and simmer using low heat for half an hour.
2. Keep sauce covered apart from when once in a while stirring.
3. Pour through coarse sieve into glass jar.
4. This sauce keeps well when placed in the fridge.

CINNAMON AND PEAR SAUCE

Time Taken: **5 minutes**

Ingredients:

- ¼ teaspoon salt
- ½ teaspoon white pepper
- 1 cup pears, seeded, chunks
- 1 tablespoon onion powder
- 1 teaspoon cinnamon powder
- 1 teaspoon garlic powder
- 2 tablespoons lemon juice
- 4 tablespoons vinegar

Directions:

1. In a blender put in all ingredients and blend well.
2. Put in to container. Enjoy.

CLASSIC COCKTAIL SAUCE

Goes great with grilled shellfish, poultry, or spicy meatballs.

Ingredients:

- ½ teaspoon Tabasco sauce
- ¾ cup chili sauce
- 1 tablespoon grated onion
- 1 tablespoon horseradish
- 1 teaspoon Worcestershire sauce
- 2 tablespoons white vinegar

Directions:

1. Mix all of the ingredients in a glass jar with a tight-fitting lid and stir to combine.
2. Store in your fridge for maximum 2 weeks.

Yield: 1 cup

CLASSIC KANSAS CITY SAUCE

Ingredients:

- ¼ cup white vinegar

- ¼ teaspoon allspice
- ¼ teaspoon cinnamon
- ¼ teaspoon mace
- ¼ teaspoon pepper
- ⅓ cup dark molasses
- ½ teaspoon chili powder
- ½ teaspoon curry powder, Oriental preferred
- ½ teaspoon hot sauce
- ½ teaspoon paprika
- 1 cup ketchup

Directions:

1. Put all the dry ingredients in a container.
2. Put in vinegar and stir. Put in the rest of the ingredients and stir until mixture is completely mixed.
3. This sauce may be served at room temperature or warmed.

Yield: 2 cups

CLASSIC SOUTHERN STYLE SAUCE

Ingredients:

- ¼ tsp. Paprika
- ¼ tsp. Tabasco
- ½ tsp. black pepper

- 1 ½ tbs. mixed whole pickling spices
- 1 beef bouillon cube
- 1 cup water
- 1 qt cider vinegar
- 1 tbs. catsup
- 1 tbs. sugar
- 2 big slices unpeeled lemon
- 2 tbs. A-1 sauce
- 2 tsp. salt
- 3 big slices unpeeled orange
- 5 tbs. Worcestershire sauce
- 6 whole mint leaves
- oregano to taste
- sweet basil and

Directions:

1. Best to cook sauce in a glass or enamel pan.
2. Mix all ingredients and simmer using low heat until orange
3. and lemon peels are well done.
4. Good sauce for pork or lamb or for basting spareribs.

CLASSIC SPICY BBQ SAUCE

Ingredients:

- ½ cup cider vinegar
- ½ cup spicy mustard
- ½ tsp. Allspice
- ½ tsp. hot sauce
- 1 cup molasses
- 1 small onion, grated
- 1 tbs. lemon juice
- 1 tsp. cayenne pepper
- 1 tsp. liquid smoke
- 2 tbs. salad oil
- 2 tsp. garlic powder
- 4 cups catsup

Directions:

1. Put ingredients in a deep cooking pan and, on moderate heat, simmer for an hour.
2. Stir frequently.

CONFETTI PEPPER CHEESE

Serve a spoonful of this colorful cream cheese mixture on top of grilled steak or chicken.

Ingredients:

- ½ teaspoon white pepper
- 1 tablespoon finely chopped jalapeño pepper

- 1 teaspoon crudely ground black pepper
- 2 cloves garlic, minced
- 2 tablespoons butter, softened
- 2 tablespoons chopped fresh chives
- 2 tablespoons chopped fresh parsley
- 2 tablespoons finely chopped red bell pepper
- 2 tablespoons finely chopped yellow bell pepper
- 2 tablespoons lemon juice
- 8 ounces light cream cheese, room temperature
- Pinch of salt

Directions:

1. Mix all of the ingredients in a small container and blend using a fork or mixer.
2. Allow the flavours to blend at least half an hour before you use. Store in your fridge for maximum one week.

Yield: 1¾ cups

CRANBERRY SAUCE

Ingredients:

- 1 can jellied cranberry sauce
- ½ small onion, grated
- 2 tbs. honey
- 2 tbs. melted butter or margarine

- 1 tbs. white wine vinegar
- 2 tsp. cornstarch
- ½ tsp. salt
- 2/3 cup white wine

Directions:

1. Mix ingredients in a deep cooking pan and simmer on moderate heat for fifteen minutes.
2. Stir once in a while.

CREAMY SAUCE FOR BARBEQUE

Time Taken: *5 minutes*

Ingredients:

- ¼ teaspoon black pepper
- ½ teaspoon cinnamon powder
- ½ teaspoon cumin powder
- 1 cup cream
- 1 cup Greek yogurt
- 1 teaspoon chili powder
- 1 teaspoon garlic powder
- 1 teaspoon onion powder
- 1 teaspoon salt

Directions:

1. In a blender put in cream with yogurt, salt, chili powder, black pepper, cinnamon powder, cumin powder, garlic powder, and onion powder.
2. Blend for a couple of times and pour into a serving dish…Enjoy.

DIJON MUSTARD AND BROWN SUGAR SAUCE

Time Taken: 5 minutes

Ingredients:

- ¼ cup apple cider vinegar
- ½ cup brown sugar
- 1 pinch salt
- 1 teaspoon garlic powder
- 2 tablespoons Dijon mustard
- 2 tablespoons soya sauce

Directions:

1. In a blender put in all ingredients and blend meticulously.
2. Enjoy.

DIPPING SAUCE FOR GRILLED VEGETABLES

Ingredients:

- ⅓ cup Dijon mustard or other dark mustard
- 1 cup mayonnaise (do not substitute low-fat or fat-free)
- 1 tablespoon lemon juice or more to thin

Directions:

1. In a small container, mix all of the ingredients.
2. Store in an airtight container in your fridge for maximum 3 weeks.

Yield: 1⅓ cups

EAST COAST SAUCE

Ingredients:

- ¼ cup brown sugar
- ½ tsp. celery salt
- ½ tsp. chili powder
- ½ tsp. dry mustard
- ½ tsp. lemon juice

- 1 clove garlic, minced
- 1 med. onion, chopped fine
- 1 tbs. Worcestershire sauce
- 1 tsp. salt
- 1/8 tsp. Pepper
- 1/8 tsp. Tabasco sauce
- 1-12oz can tomato puree
- 1-12oz can tomato sauce

Directions:

1. Mix the ingredients, in order, in a sauce pan on moderate heat.
2. Bring to its boiling point, then cover and lower heat and simmer for half an hour, stirring frequently.

EASTERN CHICKEN SAUCE

Ingredients:

- ¼ tsp. Tarragon
- ¼ tsp. thyme
- ½ cup white wine vinegar
- ½ tsp. parsley
- ½ tsp. Salt
- 1 clove garlic, minced
- 1 cup olive oil

- 1 medium onion, minced
- 1 tsp. black pepper

Directions:

1. Put mixture in glass jar and shake until well mixed.
2. Put chicken in a deep dish and pour mixture over meat.
3. Allow to stand for minimum 3 hours before grilling.

ENHANCED STORE SAUCE

Enhance your favourite store bought sauce!

Ingredients:

- ⅓ cup minced onion
- ½ cup dark brown sugar
- 2 cups of your favorite bottled barbecue sauce
- 5 big cloves garlic, minced

Directions:

1. Mix together all of the ingredients.
2. Use instantly.

Yield: 2½ cups

EZ SHELF SAUCE

Ingredients:

- ½ cup sugar
- 1 ounces. black pepper
- 1 small bottle white vinegar
- 1 small jar mustard
- 1/3 bottle hot sauce
- 2 bottles (14 oz) catsup
- 2 catsup bottles of water
- 2 ounces. garlic salt
- 2 ounces. onion salt
- 4 ounces. chili powder

Directions:

1. Mix ingredients in a deep cooking pan and bring to its boiling point.
2. Reduce heat and simmer for half an hour, stirring frequently.

FAMOUS LITTLE ROCK SAUCE

Ingredients:

- 1 ½ pints white vinegar
- 4 ounces chili powder
- ½ cup sugar, heaping
- 1-1 ounce can black pepper

- 2-24 ounce bottles catsup
- 2-24 ounce bottles water
- 1-3 ounce bottle garlic salt
- 1/3 bottle hot sauce (or more, to taste)
- 1-6 ounce jar prepared mustard

Directions:

1. Put ingredients into a deep cooking pan and bring to a rolling boil, stirring continuously.
2. Decrease the heat and simmer for half an hour, stirring frequently.
3. Store in your fridge for storage.

FIERY HOT SAUCE

Use sparingly as this sauce is too hot for most people!

Ingredients:

- ⅓ cup prepared mustard
- 1 cup (2 sticks) butter
- 1 cup cider vinegar
- 1 tablespoon cayenne pepper
- 1 tablespoon red pepper flakes

Directions:

1. In a small deep cooking pan, melt butter using low heat. Mix in vinegar, mustard, and peppers.
2. Allow the sauce to cool, then pour sauce into a glass jar with a tight-fitting lid.
3. Store in your fridge for maximum several weeks.

Yield: 2⅓ cups

FIESTA RELISH

A super versatile sauce.

Ingredients:

- ¼ cup chopped fresh cilantro
- ¼ cup chopped green onion
- ¼ cup chopped jalapeño pepper
- ¼ cup chopped tomato

Directions:

1. Mix all of the ingredients in a small container and let flavours blend at least half an hour before you use.
2. Store in your fridge for maximum 2 days.

Yield: 1 cup

FRESH CRANBERRY-ORANGE RELISH

Tastes great with smoked meats.

Ingredients:

- ¾ cup sugar
- 2 navel oranges
- 2½ cups fresh cranberries

Directions:

1. Peel the zest of the oranges and save for later. Peel away the rest of the white membrane and discard. Chop oranges and save for later. Wash and sort cranberries and save for later.
2. In a food processor with a sharp blade, mix orange zest and sugar. Pulse until zest is thoroughly ground. Put in cranberries and cut crudely. Pour mixture into a container, put in oranges, and toss. Store in your fridge for maximum 4 weeks.

Yield: 3 cups

FRUITY BBQ GLAZE

Ingredients:

- ¼ cup fruit preserves
- 1 cup of your favorite barbecue sauce

Directions:

1. Mix the ingredients in a small container.
2. Use as a glaze for pork or poultry. Store in an airtight jar in your fridge for maximum 2 months.

Yield: 1¼ cups

GALLIANO SAUCE

Ingredients:

- ¼ cup lemon juice
- ½ cup dark brown sugar
- ½ cup GALLIANO
- 1 cup chili sauce
- 2 cups catsup
- 2 tbs. Worcestershire sauce

Directions:

1. Heat ingredients in a deep cooking pan.

GARLIC AND MAYONNAISE SAUCE

Time Taken: 5 minutes

Ingredients:

- ¼ teaspoon salt
- ½ teaspoon black pepper

- 1 cup mayonnaise
- 1 tablespoon lemon juice
- 1 teaspoon garlic powder

Directions:

1. Take a container and mix mayonnaise with lemon juice, salt, pepper and garlic powder.
2. Toss thoroughly.
3. Enjoy.

GARLICKY MUSTARDAND ROSEMARY SAUCE

Time Taken: 5 minutes

Ingredients:

- ¼ teaspoon salt
- ½ teaspoon black pepper
- 1 cup balsamic vinegar
- 1 tablespoon dried rosemary
- 3 tablespoons Dijon mustard
- 5-6 garlic cloves, minced

Directions:

1. In a container put in ingredients and mix to blend.
2. Serve with desired product.

GINGERSNAP SAUCE

This is delicious with beef and red game meat.

Ingredients:

- ¼ cup cut almonds, toasted
- ¼ cup finely crushed gingersnaps
- ¼ cup raisins (not necessary)
- ⅓ cup red wine
- 1 cup au jus or brown gravy
- 1 teaspoon dark brown sugar

Directions:

1. In a small deep cooking pan, mix all of the ingredients. Simmer and stir on moderate to low heat for approximately seven minutes or until thoroughly heated.
2. Serve instantly. Store in an airtight jar in the refrigerator for maximum one week.

Yield: 2 cups

GOURMET WORCESTERSHIRE SAUCE

Time Taken: ten minutes

Ingredients:

- ½ cup tomato puree

- ½ teaspoon black pepper
- ½ teaspoon garlic powder
- 1 tablespoon onion powder
- 1 teaspoon cayenne pepper
- 1 teaspoon ginger powder
- 3 tablespoons lemon juice
- 4 tablespoons Worcestershire sauce

Directions:

1. In a container put in all ingredients and mix to blend.
2. Put in desired product in it to be marinated.
3. Cook and enjoy.

GRAPE PUNCH BBQ SAUCE

Ingredients:

- ¼ tsp. cardamom
- ¼ tsp. curry powder
- ½ tsp. black pepper
- 1 can lemonade concentrate (6 ounce, thawed)
- 1 cup grape juice (red)
- 1 tbs. salt

Directions:

1. Stir ingredients together in a container until thoroughly combined.

2. Works best on ribs.
3. Baste frequently.

GREEK ISLE RELISH

Serve alongside your favorite grilled meat. This is especially complementary with lamb.

Ingredients:

- ½ teaspoon dried oregano
- 1 big ripe tomato, finely chopped
- 1 teaspoon olive oil
- 1 teaspoon red wine vinegar
- 2 tablespoons chopped black olives
- 2 tablespoons finely chopped red onion
- 4 ounces feta cheese, crumbled

Directions:

1. Mix all of the ingredients in a glass container and stir to combine. Let marinate for minimum half an hour before you use.
2. Store in the refrigerator for maximum 3 days.

Yield: 1½ cups

GREEN CORIANDER AND MINT SAUCE

Time Taken: ten minutes

Ingredients:

- ¼ cup vinegar
- 1 bunch green coriander
- 1 bunch mint leaves
- 1 green chili
- 1 teaspoon salt
- 2 tablespoons lime juice

Directions:

1. In a blender put in coriander leaves, vinegar, mint leaves, lime juice, salt, green chili, and blend well.
2. Move into a container and serve with barbeque.

GREEN SAUCE WITH MINT AND CORIANDER

Time Taken: 5 minutes

Ingredients:

- ¼ teaspoon salt
- ½ cup ketchup
- 1 bunch coriander
- 1 bunch mint leaves
- 1 cup yogurt

- 1 green chili
- 2 garlic cloves
- 4 tablespoons soya sauce

Directions:

1. In a blender put in all ingredients and blend well.
2. Move to container.
3. Enjoy.

HARISSA SAUCE

This North African hot sauce is conventionally served with grilled lamb or kabobs.

Ingredients:

- 1 cup chopped Italian plum tomatoes, (fresh or canned)
- 1 tablespoon butter
- 1 tablespoon fresh lemon juice
- 1 tablespoon olive oil
- 1 teaspoon ground coriander
- 1½ teaspoons ground cumin
- 2 sweet red bell peppers
- 3 tablespoons chopped fresh Italian parsley
- 4 or 5 fresh hot peppers
- Salt to taste

Directions:

1. Preheat your oven to 375 degrees F. Roast the peppers by placing them in the oven for approximately twenty minutes or until they are charred and blistered. Put in a brown paper bag. Close the bag and allow peppers to steam for approximately ten minutes to loosen skins. Remove from bag. Peel, remove seeds and stems, and finely mince peppers.
2. In a moderate-sized deep cooking pan, melt butter. Put in the peppers and sauté for three to four minutes. Put in the rest of the ingredients.
3. Store in an airtight jar in your fridge for maximum 2 weeks.

Yield: 2½ cups

HAWAIIAN STYLE SAUCE

Ingredients:

- ½ cup olive oil
- 1 pint pineapple juice
- 1 tsp. dry mustard
- 2 pinches sage
- 2 pinches thyme
- 2 tbs. Worcestershire sauce
- 2 tsp. black pepper
- 4 tbs. salt

Directions:

1. Mix ingredients in deep cooking pan and bring to a slow boil.
2. Let boil for about three minutes then turn off heat.
3. Use as a baste.

HERB BUTTER

Ingredients:

- 1 cup (2 sticks) unsalted butter
- 1 tablespoon finely chopped herbs (tarragon, parsley, basil, oregano, etc.)

Directions:

1. Let butter come to room temperature. In a blender or food processor blend with herbs of your choice.
2. Store in your fridge for approximately one week or in the freezer for approximately 1 month.

Yield: 1 cup

HERB GARDEN BBQ SAUCE

Try this one with a hamburger.

Ingredients:

- 1 clove garlic, minced
- 1 cup of your favorite spicy tomato barbecue sauce
- 1 tablespoon chopped fresh parsley
- 1 teaspoon lime or lemon juice
- 4 green onions, finely chopped

Directions:

1. Mix all of the ingredients in a glass jar with a tight-fitting lid. Shake to combine.
2. Store in your fridge for maximum one week.

Yield: 1 cup

HERBED CREAM CHEESE

Ingredients:

- 1 can (4 ounces) chopped black olives
- 1 clove garlic, minced
- 1 package (8 ounces) light cream cheese, softened
- 1 tablespoon chopped fresh parsley
- 1 tablespoon snipped fresh chives
- 2 tablespoons chopped fresh basil

Directions:

1. Mix all of the ingredients and blend.

2. Serve with grilled hamburgers, sausages, or chicken as a spread for sandwiches.

Yield: 1 cup

HOISIN NO-COOK SAUCE

Ingredients:

- ¼ cup spicy prepared mustard
- 1 tbs. hot sauce
- 1 tsp. lemon peel, grated
- 2 cloves garlic, minced
- 2 cups catsup
- 2 tbs. white vinegar
- 3 tbs. Hoisin sauce
- 3 tbs. lemon juice
- 3 tbs. light corn syrup

Directions:

1. Put ingredients in glass jar,
2. Shake well, and place in fridge until ready to use.

HOLLYWOOD HAM & CHICKEN SAUCE

Ingredients:

- ¼ cup white vinegar
- 2 tbs. pickle relish
- 1 tbs. flour
- 2 tsp. sugar
- 2 tsp. Worcestershire sauce
- 1 ½ tsp. lemon juice
- 1 tsp. salt
- ¼ tsp. hot sauce
- ¼ tsp. cayenne pepper
- 2/3 cup water
- 2/3 cup butter or margarine

Directions:

1. Blend all the dry ingredients together.
2. After this, melt butter in deep cooking pan and put in the rest of the liquid ingredients and stir.
3. Put in mixed dry ingredients while stirring continuously.
4. Simmer until mixture thickens a little.
5. Pour over grilled meats.

HONEY AND MILK CHERISHED SAUCE

Time Taken: fifteen minutes

Ingredients:

- ½ cup cream

- ½ tablespoons black pepper
- 2 cups milk
- 4 tablespoons honey

Directions:

1. In a deep cooking pan put in milk and leave to boil.
2. Put in in cream and stir constantly when it reduced to half.
3. Now put in honey and mix meticulously.
4. Flavor it with pepper and turn off heat.
5. Serve with seafood and enjoy.

HONEY-JELLY BASTE

Ingredients:

- ½ cup honey
- ½ tsp. dry mustard
- 2 cups white grape jelly

Directions:

1. Put ingredients in a deep cooking pan and warm on low while stirring continuously.
2. Stir until mixture is smooth.

HOT BARBECUE GOURMET SAUCE

Time Taken: 5 minutes

Ingredients:

- ½ teaspoon cumin powder
- ½ teaspoon dry coriander powder
- 1 cup orange juice
- 1 cup soya sauce
- 1 onion, chopped
- 1 teaspoon garlic powder
- 1 teaspoon salt
- 1 teaspoon thyme
- 3-4 garlic cloves, minced
- 4 tablespoons lemon juice

Directions:

1. In a container put in all ingredients and mix thoroughly.
2. Use with chicken barbecue.

HOT CHILI GARLIC SAUCE

Time Taken: 5 minutes

Ingredients:

- ¼ teaspoon chili powder
- ½ cup vinegar
- ½ teaspoon garlic paste

- 1 cup tomato ketchup
- 1 teaspoon chili flakes
- 2 tablespoons chili sauce
- 2 tablespoons lemon juice

Directions:

1. In a container put in tomato ketchup, chili powder, chili flakes, lemon juice, chili sauce, garlic paste and vinegar.
2. Mix with fork and move into serving container.
3. Serve with desired product.

HOT LIME FISH SAUCE

Time Taken: ten minutes

Ingredients:

- ½ cup orange juice
- ½ cup vinegar
- ½ teaspoon salt
- 1 tablespoon chili sauce
- 1 tablespoons chili flakes
- 2 tablespoons lime juice

Directions:

1. Take a container and put in vinegar, chili sauce, lime juice, orange juice and mix thoroughly.

2. Put in chili flakes and salt.
3. Serve with grilled fish.

ISLAND VINAIGRETTE

A tropical baste for grilled poultry, pork, seafood, or fruits.

Ingredients:

- ⅓ cup rice wine vinegar
- ¾ cup garlic oil
- 1 tablespoon dark brown sugar
- 1 teaspoon almond extract
- 1 teaspoon minced fresh ginger
- 2 tablespoons guava juice
- 2 tablespoons orange-flavoured liqueur
- 2 tablespoons pineapple juice
- 4 basil leaves, finely cut

Directions:

1. Mix and blend vinegar, fruit juices, liqueur, brown sugar, almond extract, and ginger in a medium-size glass container. Slowly whisk in garlic oil to blend. Lightly mix in basil. Use instantly.
2. Does not keep well.

Yield: 1½ cups

JAMAICAN BBQ SAUCE

Ingredients:

- ½ teaspoon freshly ground nutmeg
- 1 clove garlic, minced
- 1 cup ketchup
- 1 onion, chopped
- 1 teaspoon allspice
- 1 teaspoon cinnamon
- 1 teaspoon freshly ground black pepper
- 1 teaspoon hot sauce
- 2 scallions, chopped
- 2 tablespoons dark brown sugar
- 2 tablespoons dark rum
- 2 tablespoons distilled vinegar
- 2 teaspoons dried thyme
- 3 tablespoons soy sauce

Directions:

1. Use a food processor to mix all of the ingredients other than the rum and process.
2. Move mixture to a big deep cooking pan and bring to its boiling point, then simmer the sauce using low heat until thick, approximately ten minutes. Mix in the rum during the last two minutes.

3. Store in an airtight jar in the refrigerator for maximum 3 weeks.

Yield: 2 cups

KAHLUA ZESTY SAUCE

Ingredients:

- ¼ cup KAHLUA
- ¼ tsp. hot sauce
- ¼ tsp. salt
- ¾ cup chili sauce
- 1 tbs. butter or margarine
- 1 tbs. Worcestershire sauce
- 1/3 cup onion, minced
- 2 tbs. brown sugar, packed

Directions:

1. Melt butter in a deep cooking pan and sauté onions until clear.
2. Stirring, pour in the remaining ingredients.
3. Simmer five minutes, stirring once in a while.

KANSAS CITY-STYLE BBQ SAUCE

Kansas City barbecue sauce is tomato-based with a sweet and tangy flavour.

Ingredients:

- ¼ cup cider vinegar
- ½ cup molasses
- ½ teaspoon salt
- 1 big onion, finely chopped
- 1 cup brown sugar
- 1 cup tomato juice
- 1 teaspoon freshly ground black pepper
- 2 cloves garlic, minced
- 2 cups ketchup
- 2 tablespoons butter
- 2 tablespoons Worcestershire sauce
- 3 or 4 dashes hot sauce

Directions:

1. In a big deep cooking pan, melt butter and sauté onion and garlic on moderate heat until translucent.
2. Put in the rest of the ingredients and simmer for an hour. Store in an airtight jar in your fridge for maximum 2 weeks.

Yield: 6 cups

KETCHUP MAYO SAUCE

Time Taken: *4 minutes*

Ingredients:

- ½ cup tomato ketchup
- ½ teaspoon chili powder
- 1 cup mayonnaise
- 1 green chili, cut
- 2 tablespoons tamarind pulp

Directions:

1. Take a container and mix all ingredients and stir thoroughly.
2. Pour into serving dish and serve with fish.

LEMON BUTTER SEAFOOD SAUCE

Time Taken: ten minutes

Ingredients:

- ½ tablespoons black pepper
- ½ teaspoon salt
- 1 cup butter
- 2 tablespoons lime juice

Directions:

1. Melt butter in a pan and put in lemon juice.
2. Stir for a minute and turn off heat.
3. Drizzle salt and pepper.
4. Pour on desired seafood.

LEMON ZEST YOGURT SAUCE

Time Taken: 5 minutes

Ingredients:

- ½ teaspoon mustard powder
- 1 cup yogurt
- 1 pinch salt
- 1 tablespoons lemon zest
- 1 teaspoon garlic powder
- 1 teaspoon white pepper

Directions:

1. In a container put in yogurt, lemon zest, mustard, garlic, salt, pepper, and mix meticulously.
2. Enjoy.

LEMON-HERB BUTTER BASTE

This is the perfect basting sauce for chicken and fish.

Ingredients:

- ¼ teaspoon fresh chopped rosemary
- ½ cup (1 stick) butter
- ½ teaspoon fresh oregano
- ½ teaspoon fresh thyme
- 1 or 2 cloves garlic, minced
- 2 tablespoons lemon juice
- Salt and white pepper to taste

Directions:

1. In a small deep cooking pan, melt butter.
2. Put in the rest of the ingredients and stir to combine.

Yield: 1 cup

LOUISIANA SAUCE

Ingredients:

- ¼ cup white wine
- ½ cup brown sugar
- ½ cup Creole mustard
- ½ cup prepared mustard
- 1 clove garlic, minced
- 3 tbs. horseradish

Directions:

1. Mix ingredients in deep cooking pan and simmer twenty minutes.
2. Stir once in a while.

LUAU HAWAIIAN SAUCE

Ingredients:

- ¼ cup salt
- 1 cup brown sugar, packed
- 1 cup vinegar
- 1 quart pineapple juice
- 2 tbs. black pepper

Directions:

1. Mix ingredients in deep cooking pan and bring to its boiling point.
2. Decrease the heat and simmer for about ten minutes.
3. Use as a baste.

MACON SAUCE

Ingredients:

- ¼ tsp. ground ginger
- 1 ½ cup catsup
- 1 cup orange juice

- 2 big onions, grated
- 2 tbs. chili powder
- 3 tbs. dark brown sugar, packed
- 3 tbs. salad oil

Directions:

1. Put ingredients in deep cooking pan and bring to its boiling point.
2. Boil for minutes then decrease the heat and simmer for an hour, stirring frequently.

MANGO AND PINEAPPLE SAUCE

Time Taken: 5 minutes

Ingredients:

- ¼ teaspoon salt
- ½ cup orange juice
- 1 cup mango, chunks
- 1 cup pineapple, chunks
- 1 teaspoon chili powder
- 1 teaspoon coriander leaves, chopped
- 1 teaspoon ginger paste

Directions:

1. In a blender put in mango chunks, orange juice, pineapple chunks, salt, chili powder, coriander, and ginger.
2. Blend till nicely pureed.
3. Move to container.

MAPLE BOURBON SAUCE

A delicious glaze for game birds and venison.

Ingredients:

- ¼ cup vegetable oil
- ½ cup bourbon
- ½ cup maple syrup
- 1 cup ketchup
- 2 tablespoons cider vinegar
- 2 tablespoons Dijon mustard

Directions:

1. In a big deep cooking pan, reduce bourbon by half on moderate to high heat.
2. Turn off the heat and put in the rest of the ingredients, stirring to combine.
3. Store in an airtight jar in the refrigerator for maximum 2 weeks.

Yield: 2¼ cups

MAYO LEMONADE SAUCE

Time Taken: 5 minutes

Ingredients:

- ¼ teaspoon black pepper
- ¼ teaspoon mustard powder
- ¼ teaspoon salt
- 1 cup mayonnaise
- 1 teaspoon garlic powder
- 3 tablespoons lime juice

Directions:

1. Take a container and put in mayonnaise, lime juice, and salt, whisk well.
2. Now put in black pepper, mustard powder, and garlic powder.
3. Stir thoroughly.
4. Pour on desired salad.
5. Enjoy.

MEDITERRANEAN DIPPING SAUCE

Makes a great bruschetta topping alongside grilled vegetables and meats.

Ingredients:

- ¼ cup freshly grated Parmesan cheese
- ¼ cup mayonnaise
- 1 clove garlic, minced
- 2 tablespoons finely chopped black olives
- 2 tablespoons finely chopped green onion
- Pinch of ground red pepper

Directions:

1. Mix all of the ingredients in a small container and allow the flavours to blend for minimum half an hour before you use.
2. Store in an airtight jar in the refrigerator for maximum 5 days.

Yield: ¾ cup

MEXENE BBQ SAUCE

Ingredients:

- ½ jar Mexene chili powder
- ½ tsp. cayenne pepper
- 1 ½ tsp. Cavender's Greek seasoning
- 1 lemon, cut
- 1 quart apple cider vinegar
- 1 quart water
- 1 tbs. dry mustard

- 1 tbs. hot sauce
- 1 tsp. Cumin
- 2 tbs. crushed red pepper 2 tbs. brown sugar
- 2 tsp. black pepper
- 3 tbs. prepared mustard
- 4 cloves garlic, minced
- 4 tbs. Worcestershire sauce

Directions:

1. Put ingredients in a deep cooking pan and bring to its boiling point, stirring once in a while.
2. Decrease the heat and simmer for about two hours, stirring once in a while.

MOM'S BBQ SAUCE

Ingredients:

- 1 big onion, finely diced
- 4 cups thick catsup
- 4 cups water
- 4 cups white vinegar
- 6 tbs. black pepper
- 6 tbs. chili powder
- 6 tbs. Salt
- 6 tbs. sugar

Directions:

1. Mix salt, sugar, black pepper and chili powder.
2. In a big pan mix catsup, vinegar, water and onion.
3. Mix in dry mixture.
4. Bring to a rolling boil, decrease the heat to low and cook uncovered for about ninety minutes, stirring every ten minutes.

MUSTARD BBQ SAUCE

Time Taken: **5 minutes**

Ingredients:

- ½ teaspoon cayenne pepper powder
- 1 cup Dijon mustard
- 1 teaspoon ginger powder
- 2 garlic cloves minced
- 3 tablespoons red wine vinegar

Directions:

1. In a container put in all ingredients and mix thoroughly.
2. Serve with grilled chicken or fish.
3. Enjoy.

MUSTARD SAUCE WITH LEMON AND GARLIC

Time Taken: 4 minutes

Ingredients:

- ¼ teaspoon salt
- ½ teaspoon garlic paste
- 1 teaspoon black pepper
- 2 tablespoon olive oil
- 2 tablespoons Dijon mustard
- 3 tablespoons lemon juice
- 4 tablespoons apple cider vinegar

Directions:

1. Mix vinegar, lemon juice, garlic paste, olive oil, mustard in a container and stir.
2. Sprinkle with salt and pepper.
3. Serve with grilled chicken or baked fish.

NEW MEXICAN COUNTRY SAUCE

Ingredients:

- ¼ cup A-1 sauce
- ½ tsp. cumin

- ½ tsp. garlic powder
- 1 tbs. chili powder
- 1 tsp. ground celery seeds
- 2 tsp. lime juice
- 2 tsp. red pepper flakes
- 2 tsp. salt
- 4 cups tomato juice

Directions:

1. Mix ingredients in a deep cooking pan and simmer using low heat for half an hour.

NEW MEXICO-STYLE BBQ SAUCE

Try this sauce with poultry or pork.

Ingredients:

- ¼ cup unsalted butter
- ¼ teaspoon cumin
- ¼ teaspoon oregano
- ½ cup red wine vinegar
- ½ cup water
- 1 red onion, finely diced
- 1 tablespoon Worcestershire sauce
- 1 teaspoon cayenne pepper
- 2 cloves garlic, finely diced

- 2 tablespoons ancho chile powder
- 2 tablespoons dark brown sugar
- 2 tablespoons pasilla chile powder
- Sea salt to taste

Directions:

1. Melt butter in a heavy frying pan using medium heat. Put in onion and garlic and sauté for approximately ten minutes until translucent.
2. Put in the rest of the ingredients and simmer for about ten minutes. Store in an airtight container in the refrigerator for one week or in the freezer for quite a few months.

Yield: 1¼ cups

NIFTY ALL MEAT SAUCE

Ingredients:

- ½ tsp. black pepper
- ½ tsp. Paprika
- ¾ cup salad oil
- ¾ cup water
- 1 can condensed tomato soup
- 1 clove garlic, minced
- 1 medium onion, chopped fine

- 1 pinch rosemary
- 1 tsp. brown sugar
- 1 tsp. dry mustard
- 1 tsp. salt
- 2 tsp. chili powder
- 2 tsp. white vinegar
- 2 tsp. Worcestershire sauce

Directions:

1. Mix ingredients in deep cooking pan and bring to its boiling point while stirring.
2. Cook for five minutes. Stir frequently.

NORTH CAROLINA DIPPING SAUCE

This vinegar-based sauce is conventionally served with chopped dry pork.

Ingredients:

- ½ cup brown sugar
- ⅔ cup ketchup
- 1 tablespoon Tabasco sauce
- 1 tablespoon Worcestershire sauce
- 1 teaspoon dry mustard
- 1 teaspoon freshly ground black pepper
- 1 teaspoon onion salt

- 1 teaspoon red pepper flakes
- 2 cups cider vinegar

Directions:

1. Mix all of the ingredients in a big deep cooking pan. Simmer for half an hour on moderate to low heat.
2. Store in an airtight jar in the refrigerator for maximum 2 weeks.

Yield: 3 cups

NORTH CAROLINA SAUCE

Ingredients:

- ¼ lb. butter or margarine
- ½ cup brown sugar, packed
- ½ cup chili powder
- ½ cup lemon juice
- ½ cup soy sauce
- ½ tsp. Worcestershire sauce
- 1 ½ cups catsup
- 1 cup prepared mustard
- 1 cup water
- 1 cup white vinegar
- 1 small clove garlic, minced
- 1 small onion, chopped fine

Directions:

1. Melt butter and put in chili powder, garlic, onion, vinegar, water, brown sugar,
2. Worcestershire sauce, soy sauce and catsup
3. Simmer for an hour
4. Put in lemon juice and mustard and simmer for fifteen minutes more

---

NUTRITIOUS BBQ SAUCE

Ingredients:

- ¼ cup cider vinegar
- ¼ tsp. black pepper
- ¼ tsp. cayenne pepper
- ¼ tsp. grated lemon peel
- 1 big onion, chopped
- 1 can peaches in water
- 1 can unsalted tomato paste (small)
- 1 can unsalted tomatoes
- 2 cloves garlic, chopped
- 2 tbs. salad oil

Directions:

1. 1 pinch each of basil, thyme and oregano

2. Mix ingredients in a blender and mix until the desired smoothness is achieved.
3. Store in covered jar in fridge.

ORANGE AND STRAWBERRY SAUCE

Time Taken: ten minutes

Ingredients:

- ¼ cup pineapple chunks
- ½ cup strawberries
- 1 pinch salt
- 1-2 garlic cloves
- 2 oranges, peeled, seeded
- 3 tablespoons brown sugar

Directions:

1. In a blender put in strawberries, oranges, pineapple chunks, garlic, salt, brown sugar and blend well.
2. Pour over your salad and enjoy.

ORANGE SHRIMP SAUCE

Ingredients:

- ½ cup orange juice

- 1 tbs. brown sugar
- 1 tbs. lemon juice
- 1 tbs. instant onion flakes
- 1 tbs. soy sauce
- ¼ tsp. salt
- 1/3 cup catsup

Directions:

1. Mix ingredients in a deep cooking pan and heat.

ORANGE-SPICE SAUCE

Ingredients:

- ¼ cup melted butter or margarine
- ¼ cup sugar
- ½ tsp. allspice
- ½ tsp. ground cloves
- 1 cup orange juice
- 2 tbs. cider vinegar
- 2 tbs. cornstarch

Directions:

1. Mix sugar, cornstarch, allspice and cloves in a deep cooking pan;
2. mix in orange juice and vinegar.

3. Over high heat while stirring continuously, bring to its boiling point for a minute.
4. Mix in butter until mixed.
5. Turn off the heat.

ORIENTAL RIB SAUCE

Ingredients:

- ¼ cup orange juice
- ½ cup dry Sherry
- ½ cup teriyaki sauce
- 1 clove garlic, minced
- 1 tbs. finely grated orange peel
- 1 tsp. black pepper
- 2 tbs. ginger
- 2 tbs. parsley, chopped fine
- 2 tsp. sesame oil

Directions:

1. Mix ingredients in shallow dish.
2. Put ribs in sauce, cover and allow it to sit overnight.
3. Bake ribs in sauce for forty minutes in a 350 degree oven.
4. Baste frequently.
5. Then cook ribs over charcoal fire for another fifteen to twenty minutes.
6. Turn and baste ribs frequently.

ORIENTAL SWEET AND SOUR PORK SAUCE

Ingredients:

- ¼ cup brown sugar, packed
- ¼ cup cider vinegar
- ½ tsp. salt
- 1 cup pineapple juice
- 1 green bell pepper, chopped fine
- 1 medium onion, chopped fine
- 1 tbs. soy sauce
- 2 tbs. cornstarch
- 2 tbs. peanut oil

Directions:

1. Mix ingredients in a deep cooking pan and bring to its boiling point.
2. Boil for about three minutes.
3. Sauce should become thick slightly.

PARSLEY AND DILL PESTO SAUCE

Time Taken: ten minutes

Ingredients:

- ¼ cup vinegar
- ¼ teaspoon salt
- 1 bunch parsley, chopped
- 1 green chili
- 1 teaspoon dill, chopped
- an inch ginger slice

Directions:

1. In a blender, put in all ingredients and blend will puree.
2. Move to serving container and serve with any seafood.
3. Enjoy.

PEACHY BBQ SAUCE

Ingredients:

- ¼ cup honey
- ¼ cup peach preserves
- ½ cup apple cider vinegar
- ½ cup Dijon mustard
- ½ cup ketchup
- ½ cup orange juice
- 1 can (7¾ ounces) cling peaches with the syrup
- 1 tablespoon dry mustard
- 1 tablespoon hot sauce
- 1 teaspoon kosher salt

- 1 teaspoon white pepper
- 6 cloves roasted garlic

Directions:

1. Use a food processor to purée the peaches and roasted garlic.
2. Pour purée together with the rest of the ingredients into a big deep cooking pan.
3. Simmer for about twenty-five minutes, stirring frequently using a wooden spoon. The mixture will become thick and be a golden, light orange. Store in a jar in the refrigerator.

Yield: 3½ cups

PEACHY KEEN SAUCE

Ingredients:

- ¼ cup catsup
- ½ tsp. liquid smoke (not necessary)
- ½ tsp. salt
- 1 med can peaches, un-drained
- 1/8 tsp. grated lemon peel
- 2 tbs. salad oil
- 3 tbs. lemon juice

Directions:

1. Put peaches and juice in blender and puree.
2. Mix the peaches with the remaining ingredients in a sauce pan
3. and, on moderate heat, simmer for fifteen minutes.
4. Do not boil.
5. It's a little different, but it is good over pork or chicken.

PEPPER BLAST BBQ SAUCE

Ingredients:

- ¼ cup salad oil
- ¾ cup brown sugar, packed
- 1 big onion, chopped
- 1 lemon, cut
- 1 tbs. prepared mustard
- 1 tsp. black pepper
- 1 tsp. cayenne pepper
- 1 tsp. flaked red pepper
- 1 tsp. hot sauce
- 2 bottle catsup
- 3 cloves garlic, chopped
- 3 cups Worcestershire sauce

Directions:

1. Mix ingredients in a deep cooking pan and simmer using low heat for about two hours, stirring frequently.

PEPPER JELLY GLAZE

Baste poultry or pork with this shiny red sauce and serve left over sauce on the side.

Ingredients:

- ¼ teaspoon dried red pepper flakes
- ½ cup apple juice
- ½ cup currant jelly or pepper jelly
- ½ teaspoon celery salt
- 2 teaspoons cornstarch

Directions:

1. In a small deep cooking pan, mix all of the ingredients and cook on moderate to high heat, stirring continuously until it boils.
2. Store in an airtight jar in your fridge for maximum 2 weeks.

Yield: 1 cup

PEPPERY SYRUP SAUCE

Ingredients:

- ¼ cup HEINZ 57 sauce
- ½ cup light corn syrup

- ½ cup white vinegar
- 1 tbs. black pepper
- 2 tsp. hot sauce

Directions:

1. Mix ingredients in a deep cooking pan and bring to its boiling point, stirring once in a while.
2. Boil for a couple of minutes, then turn off the heat.

PLUM DELICIOUS SAUCE

Ingredients:

- 1 can purple plums, pureed in blender with juice
- 1 small onion, grated
- 1 tbs. lemon juice
- 1 tsp. salt
- 3 tbs. salad oil
- 3 tbs. sugar

Directions:

1. Mix ingredients in a container and stir until well mixed.
2. Makes a truly unique baste.

QUICK & EASY NO-COOK SAUCE

Ingredients:

- ¼ tsp. celery salt
- ¼ tsp. garlic salt
- ¼ tsp. onion salt
- 1 can tomato sauce (8 ounces)
- 1 clove garlic, minced
- 1 tbs. red wine vinegar
- 2 tbs. olive oil
- 4 tbs. sherry
- 4 tsp. Worcestershire sauce

Directions:

1. Put ingredients in a big glass jar and shake like crazy.
2. Allow to stand in your fridge overnight.
3. Shake again before you serve.

QUICK ASIAN-STYLE BARBECUE SAUCE

A BBQ sauce for when you're in a rush.

Ingredients:

- 1 cup of your favorite tomato-based barbecue sauce
- 1 teaspoon ground ginger
- 1 teaspoon sesame oil
- 2 tablespoons soy sauce

Directions:

1. Mix all of the ingredients and place in your fridge.
2. Serve hot or cold, on the side, or as a baste during the final 10 to fifteen minutes of grill time.

Yield: 1 cup

QUICK MILD SAUCE

Ingredients:

- ¼ cup white vinegar
- ¾ cup melted butter or margarine
- 1 tsp. dry mustard
- 2 cups catsup
- 2 tbs. brown sugar, packed

Directions:

Put ingredients in a deep cooking pan using high heat and cook for five minutes, stirring continuously.

QUICK NO-COOK SAUCE

Ingredients:

- ¼ tsp. sugar
- 1 ½ tsp. salt

- 1 cup salad oil
- 1 jar prepared mustard (6 ounces)
- 1 tbs. cayenne pepper
- 2 bottles catsup (14 ounces)
- 2 bottles Worcestershire sauce (7 ounces)
- 2 dashes hot sauce
- 2 tbs. lemon juice
- 3 cloves garlic, pressed

Directions:

1. Mix ingredients in order in mixing container.
2. Mix thoroughly.
3. Now it's ready to serve as a baste or straight onto a sandwich.

QUICK PLUM SAUCE

Feel free to use your favourite jam instead of the one used below.

Ingredients:

- ⅛ teaspoon ground ginger
- ½ cup plum preserves or jam
- 1 clove garlic, minced
- 1 tablespoon soy sauce
- 1 tablespoon white vinegar

- Pinch of red pepper flakes

Directions:

1. In a small deep cooking pan, mix all of the ingredients. Bring mixture to its boiling point using medium heat, stirring continuously.
2. Turn off the heat and cool before you serve. Store in an airtight jar in the refrigerator for maximum several weeks.

Yield: ⅔ cup

QUICK SAUCE

Ingredients:

- ¼ cup chopped scallions
- ¼ cup lemon juice
- 1 ½ tsp. salt
- 1 dash Tabasco Sauce
- 1 tbs. brown sugar
- 1 tsp. black pepper
- 1 tsp. dry mustard
- 1/3 cup Heinz 57 Sauce
- 2 cloves of crushed garlic
- 2 cups catsup or tomato sauce
- 2 tsp. prepared mustard

Directions:

1. No cooking is necessary with this recipe.
2. Simply place everything into a blender and mix meticulously.
3. You do not necessarily need a blender.
4. You can put everything into a glass container and simply shake thoroughly until all ingredients are completely mixed.

QUICK SWEET & SPICY BBQ SAUCE

Ingredients:

- ½ teaspoon salt
- 1 big white onion, minced
- 1 cup brown sugar
- 1 cup cider vinegar
- 1 tablespoon dried thyme
- 1 teaspoon cayenne pepper
- 1 teaspoon seasoned black pepper
- 2 cups tomato sauce
- 6 tablespoons Dijon mustard

Directions:

1. In a big deep cooking pan, mix all of the ingredients. Bring to its boiling point, then lower heat and simmer for fifteen minutes to combine flavours.

2. Store in an airtight jar in your fridge for maximum 2 weeks.

Yield: 4 cups

RANCH STYLE SAUCE

Ingredients:

- ¼ cup brown sugar, packed
- ½ cup molasses
- ½ cup raisins, minced
- ½ tsp. hot sauce
- 1 cup catsup
- 1 medium onion, chopped fine
- 1 tbs. A-1 sauce
- 1 tsp. black pepper
- 1 tsp. cayenne pepper
- 1 tsp. chili powder
- 1 tsp. salt
- 2 tbs. cider vinegar

Directions:

1. Mix ingredients until completely mixed.
2. No need to cook this sauce, but tastes better if left in fridge overnight to combine flavours.

RASPBERRY BARBECUE SAUCE

An awesome glaze for grilled sausage, poultry, game, and pork.

Ingredients:

- 1 package (10 ounces) frozen raspberries
- 2 cups barbecue sauce
- 2 tablespoons brown sugar

Directions:

1. Thaw the raspberries and mix all of the ingredients in a glass jar.
2. Store in your fridge for maximum 3 weeks.

Yield: 3 cups

RASPBERRY HOT SAUCE

Time Taken: 5 minutes

Ingredients:

- ¼ cup orange concentrates
- ½ cup chili garlic sauce
- ½ cup pineapple juice
- 1 cup raspberries
- 1 teaspoon ginger paste
- 2 tablespoons brown sugar

- 2 tablespoons tomato puree
- 3 tablespoons lemon juice

Directions:

1. In blender put in raspberries with orange concentrates and pineapple juice, blend well.
2. Now put in chili garlic sauce, ginger paste, tomato puree, lemon juice and blend again for a couple of minutes.
3. Ladleinto serving container.
4. Pour over your salad and enjoy.

RASPBERRY-JALAPEÑO SAUCE

Ingredients:

- 1 bottle raspberry barbecue sauce
- 1 jalapeño, thoroughly minced, or to taste

Directions:

1. Mix the ingredients in a glass container and serve as a dipping sauce.

Yield: 1 bottle of sauce

RAW CATSUP SAUCE

Ingredients:

- ½ cup red wine vinegar
- 1 cup olive oil
- 1 med. onion, minced
- 1 tsp. black pepper
- 1 tsp. parsley
- 2 cloves garlic, minced
- 2 cups catsup
- 2 tbs. Worcestershire sauce

Directions:

1. Put ingredients in quart container with lid and shake thoroughly.
2. Put in fridge for one day.
3. Shake once in a while.

RAW HOT RIB SAUCE

Ingredients:

- ¼ cup molasses
- ¼ cup white vinegar
- ¼ tsp. black pepper
- ½ cup water
- ½ tsp. dry mustard
- 1 cup catsup
- 1 tsp. cayenne pepper

- 1 tsp. flaked red pepper
- 1 tsp. hot sauce
- 2 cloves garlic, minced
- 2 tsp. salt
- 3 tbs. Worcestershire sauce

Directions:

1. Mix ingredients in glass container and shake until well mixed.
2. Set aside and let age for ½ day.
3. Shake well before you serve.

RAW MANGO AND CORIANDER SAUCE

Time Taken: ten minutes

Ingredients:

- ½ cup yogurt
- 1 bunch coriander leaves
- 1 green chili
- 1 teaspoon cinnamon powder
- 1 teaspoon salt
- 2 raw mangoes, peeled, seeded
- 2 tablespoons lemon juice

Directions:

1. In a blender put in mango, coriander leaves, yogurt, chili, salt, lemon juice and blend well.
2. Pour into serving dish and drizzle cinnamon powder on top.
3. Serve and enjoy.

RAW MAPLE SYRUP SAUCE

Ingredients:

- ¼ cider vinegar
- ¼ cup chili sauce
- 1 ½ cups maple syrup
- 1 tsp. black pepper
- 1 tsp. dry mustard
- 2 tbs. Worcestershire sauce
- 2 tsp. salt
- 3 tbs. onions, chopped fine

Directions:

1. Mix ingredients in a container and stir until combined.

RAW TENNESSEE PIT SAUCE

Ingredients:

- ½ cup lemon juice

- ½ cup red wine vinegar
- ½ cup salad oil
- ½ tsp. monosodium glutamate
- 1 tbs. Ginger
- 1 tsp. black pepper
- 1/3 cup soy sauce
- 2 cloves garlic, mashed

Directions:

1. Put ingredients in a container and stir until well mixed.

ROASTED CUMIN YOGURT SAUCE

Time Taken: 5 minutes

Ingredients:

- 1 cup yogurt
- 1 pinch salt
- 1 tablespoon lime juice
- 1 teaspoon roasted cumin, crushed
- 3-4 mint leaves, chopped

Directions:

1. In a container put in yogurt and lime juice, stir thoroughly.
2. Now put in mint leaves and cumin, mix.

3. Enjoy.

ROASTED RED PEPPER PESTO

The flavours of this pesto are a little sweeter than a regular basil pesto. It is wonderful on pork, chicken, seafood, bruschetta, and pizza.

Ingredients:

- ¼ cup olive oil
- ¼ cup Romano cheese
- ½ cup pine nuts
- ½ teaspoon sea salt
- 1 cup packed fresh basil leaves
- 1 cup roasted red peppers
- 1 teaspoon black pepper
- 8 cloves garlic, minced

Directions:

1. Use a food processor to mix red peppers, basil, pine nuts, garlic, pepper, and salt. Process by pulsating for approximately 20 to half a minute to finely cut ingredients.
2. Then put in oil and process for another fifteen seconds to make a paste. Move to a container and mix in the cheese.
3. Chill until ready to serve.

4. Does not keep well.

Yield: 2 cups

ROCK HOUSE SAUCE

Ingredients:

- ¼ cup melted butter or margarine
- ½ cup catsup
- ½ cup white vinegar
- ½ tsp. chili powder
- ½ tsp. hot sauce
- 1 ½ cups water
- 1 ½ tsp. salt
- 1 big onion, minced
- 1 clove garlic, minced
- 1 cup Worcestershire sauce
- 1 tbs. dry mustard
- 1 tsp. sugar

Directions:

1. Put ingredients in deep cooking pan and bring to its boiling point.
2. Decrease the heat and simmer for fifteen minutes.

ROSEMARY AND CHILI LIME SAUCE

Time Taken: 5 minutes

Ingredients:

- ½ teaspoon dry coriander powder
- 1 tablespoon chili flakes
- 1 tablespoons rosemary, chopped
- 1 teaspoon garlic powder
- 1 teaspoon salt
- 2 tablespoons apple cider vinegar
- 2 tablespoons Dijon mustard
- 4 tablespoons lime juice

Directions:

1. In a container put in mustard, salt, chili flakes, vinegar, lime juice, coriander powder, and rosemary and garlic powder.
2. Mix thoroughly.

ROSEMARY BUTTER

Serve atop grilled meats and vegetables.

Ingredients:

- ½ cup (1 stick) butter, room temperature

- 1 clove garlic, minced
- 2 teaspoons crushed rosemary
- Cracked pepper to taste

Directions:

1. Whip butter with rosemary, garlic, and pepper.
2. Cover butter using plastic wrap and mould into a log. Store in the freezer for quite a few months.
3. To serve, slightly thaw and slice.

Yield: ½ cup

ROUILLE

A tomato-and-red-pepper-flavoured French mayonnaise that is conventionally served with fish soup.

Ingredients:

- ¼ teaspoon freshly ground black pepper
- ½ teaspoon sea salt
- 1 cup olive oil
- 1 fresh serrano chile pepper, cored, seeded, and minced
- 2 teaspoons sun-dried tomato paste
- 4 fresh organic egg yolks
- 4 to 6 cloves garlic, minced

Directions:

1. Use a food processor to mix egg yolks, garlic, chile pepper, tomato paste, salt, and pepper.
2. Slowly put in olive oil to blend. Store in your fridge for maximum 3 days.

Yield: 1¼ cups

SANDWICH SAUCE

Ingredients:

- ¼ cup white vinegar
- ¼ tsp. marjoram
- ½ tsp. celery salt
- 1 big onion, minced
- 1 can tomato sauce
- 1 clove garlic, minced
- 1 tsp. dry mustard
- 2 bay leaves, crumbled
- 2 tbs. salad oil
- 2 tsp. chili powder

Directions:

1. Put salad oil, onions and garlic in a deep cooking pan and cook for five minutes,
2. then put in the remaining ingredients and simmer for about forty-five minutes.

3. Stir ingredients frequently and do not allow to boil.
4. This sauce is best served poured over a sandwich or slices of meat.
5. Serve warm.

SECRET FINISHING SAUCE

Ingredients:

- ¼ cup cider vinegar
- ¼ cup fresh grapefruit juice
- ¼ cup tightly packed dark brown sugar
- ½ cup olive oil
- ½ teaspoon cayenne pepper
- 1 can (6 ounces) tomato paste
- 1 tablespoon capers
- 2 tablespoons prepared horseradish

Directions:

1. Use a food processor to mix vinegar, grapefruit juice, brown sugar, tomato paste, horseradish, capers, and cayenne.
2. Slowly put in oil in a thin stream and continue to pulse until well mixed.
3. May be used as a marinade, basting sauce, or serving sauce. Store in an airtight container in your fridge for maximum 3 days.

Yield: 2 cups

SESAME SOY SAUCE

Enjoy with chicken and pork satay.

Ingredients:

- ⅓ cup soy sauce
- ½ teaspoon five-spice powder
- ⅔ cup rice vinegar
- 1 teaspoon sesame oil
- 2 cloves garlic, minced

Directions:

1. Mix all of the ingredients in a glass container and serve as a dipping sauce.

Yield: 1 cup

SESAME-CITRUS SAUCE

Goes great with seafood.

Ingredients:

- ½ cup plain yogurt
- ½ cup tahini (sesame paste)

- ½ teaspoon Tabasco sauce or to taste
- 1 lime, quartered for decoration
- 1 tablespoon lemon juice
- 1 tablespoon lime juice
- 1 tablespoon rice vinegar
- 1 teaspoon toasted sesame seeds for decoration
- 2 cloves garlic, minced

Directions:

1. Mix all of the ingredients, saving for later the lime quarters and sesame seeds. Squeeze lime quarters over grilled fish.
2. Ladle sauce over fish and drizzle with a few sesame seeds for decoration. Store in your fridge for maximum a few days.

Yield: 1½ cups

SHERRY CHICKEN SAUCE

Ingredients:

- 1 cup salad oil
- 1 cup sherry
- 1 medium onion, grated
- 1 tsp. salt
- 2 cloves garlic, minced

- 2 tbs. lemon juice
- 2 tbs. Mayonnaise
- 3 tbs. Worcestershire sauce
- 3 tsp. black pepper
- 3 tsp. thyme

Directions:

1. Blend ingredients in a blender until thoroughly combined.
2. Baste chicken frequently.

SHISH KEBAB HONEY SAUCE

Ingredients:

- ½ cup olive oil
- ½ tsp. Oregano
- ½ tsp. rosemary, crushed
- 1 can tomato paste
- 1 cup dry white wine
- 1 cup honey
- 1 tsp. salt
- 2 cloves garlic, mashed

Directions:

1. Mix ingredients in a container.
2. Yes, it can be used on meats other than shish kebabs.
3. Baste meat and veggies frequently.

SHRIMP BBQ SAUCE

Sprinkle this sauce over a grilled shrimp salad.

Ingredients:

- ¼ cup Italian salad dressing
- ¼ cup of your favorite barbecue sauce

Directions:

1. Mix the ingredients in a glass container and use to marinate shrimp for half an hour.

Yield: ½ cup

SIMPLE SATAY SAUCE

It goes well with poultry and pork, too.

Ingredients:

- 2 tablespoons soy sauce
- 4 cloves garlic, minced
- 4 tablespoons fresh lime juice

Directions:

1. Mix all of the ingredients in a small glass container.
2. You can make this recipe in bigger quantities and store in your fridge for maximum one week.

Yield: ⅓ cup

SIZZLING APPLE CIDER BBQ SAUCE

Time Taken: 5 minutes

Ingredients:

- ½ cup tomato ketchup
- ½ cup tomato sauce
- 1 cup apple cider vinegar
- 1 teaspoon chili powder
- 1 teaspoon garlic powder
- 1 teaspoon salt
- 2 tablespoons lemon juice

Directions:

1. In a container put in all ingredients and mix thoroughly.
2. Serve with steak or grilled lamb.

SIZZLING BBQ SAUCE

Ingredients:

- ½ cup flour
- ½ cup salad oil
- ½ cup white vinegar

- ½ tsp. black pepper
- ½ tsp. hot sauce
- ½ tsp. liquid smoke
- ½ tsp. powdered garlic
- 1 cup water
- 1 tbs. salt
- 1 tsp. dry mustard
- 2 medium onions, minced

Directions:

1. Mix ingredients in deep cooking pan and bring to its boiling point.
2. Decrease the heat and simmer for about ten minutes.
3. Serve hot.

SIZZLING CHILI CIDER SAUCE

Time Taken: ten minutes

Ingredients:

- ¼ cup vinegar
- ½ teaspoon salt
- 1 cup apple cider vinegar
- 1 garlic clove, minced
- 1 green chili, cut
- 1 red chili, cut

Directions:

1. In a container put in vinegar, garlic, apple cider vinegar, red chilies, green chilies, salt and place into thefridge for about forty minutes.
2. Serve with baked fish.

SMOKEY CHIPOTLE SAUCE

Ingredients:

- ¼ cup balsamic vinegar
- ¼ cup brown sugar
- ¼ cup lemon juice
- ½ cup sour purée bourbon
- 1 clove garlic, minced
- 1 cup boiling water
- 1 cup ketchup
- 1 onion, finely chopped
- 1 tablespoon ancho chile powder
- 2 tablespoons butter
- 2 tablespoons Worcestershire sauce
- 2 teaspoons dry mustard
- 4 dried chipotle chiles

Directions:

1. Wash chiles. Pour boiling water over chiles and allow them to rehydrate and tenderize for half an hour, then drain.
2. In a big deep cooking pan, melt butter and sauté onion and garlic on moderate heat until tender.
3. Then put in bourbon, lower heat to a simmer, and reduce to half. Put in chiles and the rest of the ingredients, bring to its boiling point, then decrease the heat and simmer for minimum 1 hour. Purée sauce in a blender until the desired smoothness is achieved.
4. Store in an airtight container in your fridge for 3 to 4 weeks or in the freezer for quite a few months.

Yield: 3 cups

SMOKEY WHISKEY SAUCE

Ingredients:

- 1 cup onions, minced
- ½ cup cider vinegar
- ½ cup orange juice
- ½ cup maple syrup
- 1 stick butter or margarine
- 2 tbs. Worcestershire sauce
- 1 tbs. grated orange peel
- 1 tsp. black pepper

- 1/3 cup salad oil
- 1/3 cup sorghum molasses
- 2/3 cup catsup
- 2/3 cup bourbon or sour purée whiskey

Directions:

1. Put ingredients in a deep cooking pan and bring to a simmer while stirring frequently.
2. Simmer for an hour, until thick and shiny.
3. Stir frequently.

SOUTH OF THE BORDER SAUCE

Ingredients:

- ¼ cup onion, minced
- ¼ cup ripe olives, chopped fine
- ½ cup olive oil
- ½ tsp. hot sauce
- 1 beef bouillon cube
- 1 can tomato sauce
- 1 clove garlic, minced
- 1 tbs. butter or margarine
- 1 tbs. chili powder
- 2/3 cup water

Directions:

1. In a deep cooking pan, sauté onions and garlic in the olive oil and butter.
2. Put in rest of the ingredients and simmer, on moderate heat, for half an hour.

SOUTHWESTERN CITRUS BARBECUE SAUCE

Ingredients:

- ½ cup lime juice
- ½ teaspoon ground red pepper
- ½ teaspoon salt
- 1 big white onion, chopped
- 1 cup orange juice
- 1 tablespoon snipped fresh cilantro
- 1 tablespoon vegetable oil
- 2 tablespoons brown sugar

Directions:

1. Heat oil in a big sauté pan, put in onion and sauté for about five minutes. Mix in the rest of the ingredients.
2. Bring to its boiling point, then decrease the heat to low, and simmer uncovered for about fifteen minutes, stirring once in a while. Store in the refrigerator for maximum 3 days.

Yield: 2 cups

SOY AND WINE SAUCE

Ingredients:

- ¼ cup burgundy or concord wine
- ¼ cup dark brown sugar, packed
- 1 ½ cups water
- 1 bottle soy sauce (5 ounce)
- 1 tbs. lemon juice
- 1 tsp. Worcestershire sauce

Directions:

1. Blend ingredients until sugar dissolves.
2. Baste frequently with this sauce for full effect.

SOYA HOT GINGERY SAUCE

Time Taken: 5 minutes

Ingredients:

- ½ tablespoons black pepper
- ½ teaspoon salt
- 1 cup soya sauce
- 1 teaspoon ginger paste

- 2 garlic cloves, minced

Directions:

1. Take a container and put in soya sauce, ginger, garlic and mix thoroughly.
2. Sprinkle with salt and pepper.
3. Serve.

SOYA ONION BARBECUE SAUCE

Time Taken: 5 minutes

Ingredients:

- ¼ cup apple cider vinegar
- ¼ teaspoon salt
- ½ cup soya sauce
- 1 onion, chopped
- 1 teaspoon black pepper
- 1 teaspoon dried basil
- 2 tablespoons soya sauce
- 2 tablespoons Worcestershire sauce

Directions:

1. In a container put in all ingredients and mix thoroughly.
2. Enjoy.

SPECIAL BEEF SAUCE

Ingredients:

- ¼ cup minced onion 1 clove garlic, minced
- ½ cup salad oil
- ½ tsp. black pepper
- ½ tsp. Paprika
- ¾ tsp. salt
- 1 ¼ cup tomato juice
- 1 cup catsup
- 1 tbs. sugar
- 1 tbs. Worcestershire sauce
- 2 dashes Tabasco
- 2 tsp. horseradish
- 3 tbs. white vinegar

Directions:

1. Mix all ingredients in pot and simmer over moderate low heat for half an hour.

SPECIAL HOT AND SPICY SAUCE

Ingredients:

- 3 cups chili sauce
- ¼ cup cider vinegar

- 2 tbs. dry mustard
- 2 tbs. Worcestershire sauce
- 1 tbs. hot sauce
- 1 tsp. cayenne pepper
- 1 tsp. black pepper
- 2/3 cup apple jelly

Directions:

1. Mix ingredients in a deep cooking pan and bring to its boiling point, stirring frequently.
2. Decrease the heat and simmer for about ten minutes.
3. Allow to cool.

SPICY HORSERADISH SAUCE

Try this with plain meats and fish like chicken, game hens, catfish, and shellfish.

Ingredients:

- ½ teaspoon coriander
- ½ teaspoon red pepper flakes
- 1 cup light sour cream
- 1 tablespoon paprika
- 1 teaspoon allspice
- 1 teaspoon ground cumin
- 2 tablespoons chopped pimiento

- 4 tablespoons horseradish

Directions:

1. Mix all of the ingredients in a glass container. Place in the refrigerator for an hour before you serve.
2. Store in the refrigerator for maximum 3 days.

Yield: 1½ cups

SPICY KETCHUP-MUSTARD SAUCE

Goes great with grilled pork and French fries!

Ingredients:

- 1 cup ketchup
- 1 teaspoon curry powder
- 2 tablespoons cider vinegar
- 2 tablespoons dry mustard

Directions:

1. Mix all of the ingredients in a glass jar with a tight-fitting lid.
2. Store in your fridge for maximum 4 weeks.

Yield: 1¼ cups

SPICY ORANGE SAUCE

Ingredients:

- ¼ cup peanut oil
- ¼ tsp. cayenne pepper
- ½ tsp. cinnamon
- ½ tsp. ground cloves
- ½ tsp. liquid smoke
- 1 ½ cups chili sauce
- 1 big onion, minced
- 1 cup orange marmalade
- 1 tbs. ground ginger
- 1 tbs. sesame oil
- 1 tsp. black pepper
- 1/3 cup red wine vinegar
- 3 cloves garlic, minced
- 3 tbs. soy sauce

Directions:

1. Put ingredients in deep cooking pan and bring to its boiling point, stirring continuously.
2. Decrease the heat and simmer until shiny, stirring frequently. (about fifteen minutes)
3. Turn off the heat.

SPICY SHRIMP BASTING SAUCE

Ingredients:

- ¼ cup chili sauce
- ½ tsp. hot sauce
- 1 cup olive oil
- 1 tsp. lemon juice
- 1 tsp. oregano
- 1 tsp. salt
- 2 cloves garlic, mashed

Directions:

1. Mix ingredients until well mixed.
2. Brush on shrimp frequently while cooking.
3. You might try soaking shrimp in this mixture for about 1 hour or two before grilling, then use as baste also.

SPICY VINEGAR SAUCE

Ingredients:

- ⅓ cup crushed red pepper flakes
- ⅓ cup sugar
- 1 quart white vinegar
- 1½ tablespoons sea salt

Directions:

1. Mix all of the ingredients in a glass container and allow it to stand at room temperature for quite a few hours for flavours to combine.
2. Pour into a plastic squirt bottle. Store indefinitely in your fridge.

Yield: 1 quart

STEAK SEASONING BBQ SAUCE

Ingredients:

- ¼ cup Blue cheese salad dressing
- ¼ cup Worcestershire sauce
- ½ cup bacon grease
- ½ cup brown sugar, packed
- ½ cup catsup
- ½ stick butter or margarine
- 1 beer
- 1 lemon, cut in half
- 1 tbs. hot sauce
- 2 tbs. dried onions
- 2 tsp. prepared mustard
- 5 shakes steak seasoning

Directions:

1. Mix all but the final 2 ingredients in a deep cooking pan.

2. Squeeze lemon into mixture, then throw in the lemon.
3. Simmer using low heat for about twenty minutes.
4. Use beer to thin mixture. (about ½ can)
5. Drink the rest.
6. Stir sauce once in a while.

SUGARY BARBECUE CHILI SAUCE

Time Taken: 5 minutes

Ingredients:

- ½ cup brown sugar
- ½ cup soya sauce
- ½cup apple cider vinegar
- 1 teaspoon garlic powder
- 1 teaspoon salt
- 1 teaspoon tablespoons chili flakes

Directions:

1. In a container put in all ingredients and stir thoroughly till sugar is dissolved.
2. Enjoy.

SUPERHOT BBQ SAUCE

Ingredients:

- 1 bottle catsup
- 1 stick butter or margarine
- 1 tbs. Lea & Perrins sauce
- 2 cloves garlic, minced
- 3 tbs. liquid smoke
- 3 tbs. Worcestershire sauce

Directions:

1. In a deep cooking pan, simmer garlic in the butter for five minutes.
2. Put in rest of ingredients and simmer, on moderate heat, for about twenty minutes.
3. Stir once in a while.

SWEET 'N SPICY BBQ SAUCE

Ingredients:

- ⅓ cup brown sugar, packed
- ⅓ cup orange juice
- ½ cup Worcestershire sauce
- ½ teaspoon liquid smoke
- 1 cup beef bouillon
- 1 cup chili sauce
- 1 cup ketchup

- 1 onion, chopped
- 1 teaspoon Tabasco sauce or to taste
- 2 cloves garlic, minced

Directions:

1. Mix all of the ingredients in a big deep cooking pan.
2. Simmer uncovered using low heat for about forty-five minutes to reduce sauce.
3. Serve hot or cold.

Yield: 4 cups

SWEET AND SOUR BARBECUE SAUCE

Ingredients:

- 1 ½ cups red wine vinegar
- ¼ cup soy sauce
- 1 cup brown sugar, packed
- 2 cans frozen pineapple juice concentrate
- 2 tsp. salt
- 3 cloves garlic, minced
- ½ green bell pepper, chopped fine
- 1/3 cup salad oil

Directions:

1. Put ingredients in a deep cooking pan and simmer ten minutes on moderate heat.
2. Baste meats frequently.

SWEET AND SOUR CORIANDER SAUCE

Time Taken: ten minutes

Ingredients:

- ¼ teaspoon salt
- 1 bunch fresh coriander, chopped
- 1 cup sour cream
- 1 green chili
- 2 tablespoons apple cider vinegar
- 2 tablespoons sugar
- 4 tablespoons lemon juice

Directions:

1. In a blender put in sour cream with coriander, salt, chili, sugar, lemon juice, vinegar, and blend till puree.
2. Move into serving container.
3. Pour over your salad and enjoy.

SWEET AND SOUR MUSTARD SAUCE

Time Taken: 5 minutes

Ingredients:

- ¼ cup brown sugar
- ¼ teaspoon chili powder
- ½ cup tomato ketchup
- ½ teaspoon garlic paste
- 2 tablespoons chili sauce
- 2 tablespoons Dijon mustard
- 3 tablespoons apple cider vinegar

Directions:

1. In a container put in ingredients and mix to blend.
2. Serve with desired product.

SWEET AND SOUR ORIENTAL BASTE

Ingredients:

- ½ small onion, grated
- ½ tsp. garlic salt
- ¾ cup red wine (port)
- 1 can crushed pineapple in its sauce
- 1 tbs. brown sugar, packed
- 1 tbs. soy sauce
- 1 tsp. lemon juice
- 2 tbs. salad oil
- 3 tbs. red wine vinegar

Directions:

1. Mix ingredients in a deep cooking pan and simmer on moderate heat for about twenty minutes.

SWEET AND SOUR SYRUP SAUCE

Ingredients:

- ¼ cup plus 2 tbs. white vinegar
- ½ tsp. salt
- 1 cup corn syrup
- 1 tbs. plus 1 tsp. Worcestershire sauce
- 2 tbs. dry mustard

Directions:

1. Mix ingredients in a container and stir until well mixed.
2. Baste meats frequently.

SWEET BARBECUE ONION SAUCE

Time Taken: 5 minutes

Ingredients:

- ¼ teaspoon salt
- ½ cup honey
- ½ cup ketchup

- 1 teaspoon black pepper, crushed
- 1 teaspoon garlic powder
- 2 tablespoons brown sugar
- 2tablespoonsonion powder
- 4 tablespoons soya sauce

Directions:

1. In a container put in all ingredients and mix meticulously.
2. Enjoy.

SWEET TANGY ORIENTAL SAUCE

Ingredients:

- ¼ cup light molasses
- ¼ cup soy sauce ¼ cup salad oil
- ½ tsp. celery seed
- 1 can frozen orange juice, thawed (6 ounces)
- 1 tsp. dry mustard
- 1 tsp. garlic powder
- 1 tsp. ground ginger
- 1 tsp. minced green onion
- 1 tsp. minced onion

Directions:

1. Mix ingredients in a deep cooking pan and simmer on
   moderate heat for about ten minutes.

2. Use sauce to baste meats frequently.

SWIFT HORSERADISH SAUCE

Serve this creamy, mild sauce with grilled or smoked beef.

Ingredients:

- 2 cups whipped cream
- 2 tablespoons horseradish

Directions:

1. Blend together whipped cream and horseradish.
2. Place in your fridge until ready to serve.

Yield: 2 cups

SZECHUAN SAUCE

This hot sauce is best enjoyed with seafood.

Ingredients:

- ¼ cup dry vermouth
- ¼ cup rice vinegar
- ¼ cup soy sauce
- ½ cup honey, warmed
- 1 cup bottled Szechuan sauce

- 1 tablespoon minced ginger

Directions:

1. Mix all of the ingredients in a glass jar with a tight-fitting lid and shake to combine.
2. Store in your fridge for maximum several weeks.

Yield: 2 cups

TAHITIAN BBQ SAUCE

Ingredients:

- ¼ cup apricot or peach preserves
- ¼ cup catsup
- ¼ cup pineapple preserves
- 1 tsp. ground ginger
- 1/3 cup teriyaki sauce

Directions:

1. Mix ingredients in a container.
2. There is no need to cook this sauce.
3. Baste meat frequently.

TAMARIND SAUCE WITH BROWN SUGAR

Time Taken: ten minutes

Ingredients:

- ¼ cup water
- ½ teaspoon black pepper
- ½ teaspoon salt
- 1 cup tamarind pulp
- 2 tablespoons white vinegar
- 3 tablespoons brown sugar
- 3 tablespoons soya sauce

Directions:

1. Take a blender and fill with tamarind pulp, brown sugar, soya sauce, salt, water, vinegar, and pepper, blend well.
2. Serve with baked fish.

TANGERINE GLAZE

Ingredients:

- 1 can (6 ounces) tangerine juice
- 1 teaspoon minced fresh ginger
- 2 tablespoons dark honey
- 2 tablespoons teriyaki sauce
- 3 ounces frozen pineapple juice concentrate

Directions:

1. Mix all of the ingredients in a glass jar and blend well. Glaze meats during the final ten minutes of grilling, or fish during the last five minutes of grilling.
2. Store in your fridge for maximum 2 weeks.

Yield: 1¼ cups

TANGY APRICOT SAUCE

Goes great with all types of poultry and pork.

Ingredients:

- 1 jar (12 ounces) apricot preserves
- 1 tablespoon soy sauce
- 2 tablespoons rice vinegar

Directions:

1. Mix all of the ingredients.

Yield: 1½ cups

TANGY CATSUP BBQ SAUCE

Ingredients:

- 1 cup white vinegar
- 1 pint catsup

- 1 pint water
- 2 ¼ tbs. black pepper
- 2 ¼ tbs. chili powder
- 2 ¼ tbs. salt
- 2 ¼ tbs. sugar
- 2 tbs. onion, chopped fine

Directions:

1. Mix ingredients in a deep cooking pan and simmer for about two hours.
2. Stir frequently

TENNESSEE SAUCE

Ingredients:

- ¼ cup flour
- ¼ cup salt
- ½ tsp. basil
- ½ tsp. thyme
- 1 pound okra, chopped fine
- 1 quart cider vinegar
- 1 tbs. black pepper
- 1 tbs. flaked red pepper
- 2 medium onions, grated
- 2 sticks butter or margarine

- 2 tsp. hot sauce
- 5 pounds whole ripe tomatoes

Directions:

1. Mix ingredients in deep cooking pan and bring to its boiling point.
2. Decrease the heat to low and simmer for half an hour, then strain mixture through a coarse sieve.
3. Use sauce for basting and serving over meat.

TEXAN BEEF BRISKET SERVING SAUCE

Ingredients:

- ¼ cup brown sugar
- 1 big onion, chopped
- 1 cup chili sauce
- 1 teaspoon dry mustard
- 1 teaspoon ground black pepper
- 2 cups tomato sauce
- 2 tablespoons apple cider vinegar
- 2 tablespoons olive oil
- 2 tablespoons Worcestershire sauce
- 2 teaspoons cayenne pepper
- 3 cloves garlic, minced

Directions:

1. Heat oil in a big sauté pan. Put in onion and garlic and cook on moderate to high heat for approximately 7 to ten minutes, until mildly browned. Mix in the rest of the ingredients and bring to its boiling point.
2. Decrease the heat and simmer for an hour. Strain sauce and discard solids. Store in an airtight jar in the refrigerator for quite a few weeks.

Yield: 4 cups

TEXAS PECOS STYLE SAUCE

Ingredients:

- ½ tsp. cayenne pepper
- 1 ½ tbs. dark brown sugar
- 1 ½ tsp. powdered mustard
- 1 cup distilled vinegar
- 1 ounce tequila
- 1 pinch granulated jalapeno peppers
- 1 tbs. salt
- 1 tbs. white corn syrup
- 1 tsp. liquid smoke
- 2 qt. tomato sauce
- 4 pickled Louisiana peppers, chopped fine
- 5 cups water

Directions:

1. Put ingredients in a big pot and bring to its boiling point while stirring.
2. Decrease the heat and simmer for approximately 2 hours, stirring once in a while.
3. This sauce can be used as a baste or just poured over the meat.

THAI PEANUT DIPPING SAUCE

Try this sauce with grilled pork tenderloin, lamb, or chicken.

Ingredients:

- ¼ cup crispy peanut butter
- ¼ cup rice wine vinegar
- ¼ cup soy sauce
- ½ teaspoon ground ginger
- 1 teaspoon sesame oil
- 2 tablespoons brown sugar

Directions:

1. Mix all of the ingredients in a glass container and whisk to combine.
2. Store in an airtight jar in your fridge for maximum 3 weeks.

Yield: ¾ cup

THAI SERVING SAUCE

Try with lamb, pork, and poultry.

Ingredients:

- ½ cup chopped green onions
- ½ cup chopped peanuts
- ½ cup coconut milk
- ½ cup Dijon mustard
- ½ cup peanut butter

Directions:

1. Mix all of the ingredients and use as a serving sauce.
2. Store in an airtight container in your fridge for maximum 2 weeks.

Yield: 2½ cups

THREE-PEPPER BUTTER

Ingredients:

- ¼ teaspoon red pepper
- ¼ teaspoon sea salt
- ½ cup (1 stick) butter, softened
- ½ teaspoon paprika
- 1 fresh red New Mexican chile, minced

- 1 tablespoon minced red onion

Directions:

1. In a small container, mix all of the ingredients and meticulously blend. Put butter on a square of plastic wrap and mould into a log the size of a big coin.
2. Put in a sealable freezer bag for storage. Slice pats of the butter when ready to serve. Store in the freezer for maximum three months.

Yield: ½ cup

TIA MARIA BBQ SAUCE

Ingredients:

- ¼ cup honey
- ¼ cup soy sauce
- ½ cup TIA MARIA
- 1 can tomato paste
- 1 chicken bouillon cube
- 1 cup water
- 1 tsp. black pepper
- 2 cloves garlic, minced
- 2 tsp. salt

Directions:

1. Put ingredients in a deep cooking pan and heat.
2. Stir continuously until all ingredients are mixed, then remove from fire.

TOMATO KETCHUP AND DATE SAUCE

Time Taken: *5 minutes*

Ingredients:

- ½ teaspoon cumin seeds
- 1 cup tomato ketchup
- 1 teaspoon chili powder
- 2 cups dates, seeded, soaked
- 2 red chilies
- 2 tablespoons lemon juice
- 4-5 garlic cloves

Directions:

1. In a blender put in dates, lemon juice, cumin seeds, garlic, chili powder, red chilies and blend well.
2. Move into a container and put in ketchup, stir until blended.
3. Serve with desired product.

TOMATO SAUCE WITH CHILIES

Time Taken: ten minutes

Ingredients:

- ½ tablespoons chili powder
- ½ teaspoon ground black pepper
- ½ teaspoon salt
- 1 teaspoon garlic paste
- 2 green chilies, chopped
- 2 tablespoons lime juice
- 2 tablespoons olive oil
- 2 tomatoes, chopped

Directions:

1. Heat oil in pan and fry onion for a minute.
2. Put in tomatoes and chilies, fry for five minutes.
3. Sprinkle with salt, black pepper, and chili powder.
4. Serve with desired seafood.

TOMATO SOUP SAUCE

Ingredients:

- ¼ cup salad oil
- ¼ cup sugar
- ½ green bell pepper, chopped fine
- 1 can condensed tomato soup
- 1 can water

- 1 medium onion, chopped fine
- 1 tbs. chili powder
- 1 tsp. liquid smoke
- 1/3 cup white vinegar

Directions:

1. Mix ingredients in a deep cooking pan and bring to its boiling point.
2. Decrease the heat and simmer for about twenty minutes.
3. Stir frequently.

TOMATO-BEER BASTING SAUCE

Ingredients:

- ¼ cup cider vinegar
- ½ tsp. black pepper
- 1 ½ cups tomato puree
- 1 ½ tsp. salt
- 1 cup beer
- 1 tsp. paprika
- 2 dashes hot sauce
- 3 tbs. Worcestershire sauce

Directions:

1. Put ingredients in a deep cooking pan and, using low heat,

2. simmer for about ten minutes.

TRADITIONAL RASPBERRY BBQ SAUCE

Time Taken: ten minutes

Ingredients:

- ¼ teaspoon salt
- 1 cup raspberries
- 1 teaspoon chili powder
- 1 teaspoon garlic paste
- 1 teaspoon mustard powder
- 2 tablespoons honey
- 4 tablespoons soya sauce

Directions:

1. In a blender put in all ingredients and blend till smooth.
2. Use with meat or chicken.
3. Enjoy.

TRIPLE RED PEPPER SAUCE

This is a beautiful bright red salsa that packs a kick of heat.

Ingredients:

- ½ tablespoon red pepper flakes

- 1 can (10 ounces) diced Rotel tomatoes
- 1 red bell pepper, roasted and finely chopped
- 1 teaspoon Tabasco or your favorite hot sauce
- 2 teaspoons cayenne pepper
- 3 tablespoon lemon juice

Directions:

1. Put all of the ingredients in a big deep cooking pan.
2. Simmer for approximately fifteen to twenty minutes using low heat.
3. Serve as a hot and spicy side sauce for the meat of your choice. Store in an airtight jar in your fridge for maximum 2 weeks.

Yield: 1½ cups

TROPIC TAMARIND SAUCE

Time Taken: **5 minutes**

Ingredients:

- ½ teaspoon cinnamon powder
- ½ teaspoon cumin powder
- 1 cup tamarind pulp
- 1 teaspoon chili powder
- 1 teaspoon salt
- 2 tablespoons vinegar

Directions:

1. Take a container and put in tamarind pulp, vinegar, cumin powder, cinnamon powder and sprinkle with salt and pepper.
2. Pour into serving dish and serve with chickenbarbeque.
3. Enjoy.

TURMERIC AND YOGURT BBQ SAUCE

Time Taken: 4 minutes

Ingredients:

- ¼ teaspoon turmeric powder
- 1 cup yogurt
- 1 tablespoons onion powder
- 1 teaspoon black pepper
- 1 teaspoon garlic powder
- 1 teaspoon ginger powder
- 2 tablespoons lime juice

Directions:

1. Take a container and put in all ingredients.
2. Toss to blend well.
3. Serve with your desired produce.
4. Enjoy.

ULTIMATE ALL PURPOSE SAUCE

Ingredients:

- ¼ cup brown sugar, packed
- 1 big onion, chopped fine
- 1 cup catsup
- 1 cup water
- 2 tbs. butter or margarine
- 2 tbs. dark vinegar
- 2 tsp. dry mustard
- 3 tbs. Worcestershire sauce

Directions:

1. Melt butter in deep cooking pan and put in onion.
2. Cook until onions are clear then put in rest of ingredients.
3. Simmer the final mixture for fifteen minutes.

ULTIMATE PORK SAUCE

Ingredients:

- ½ cup water
- ½ tsp. paprika
- 1 ½ cups tomato sauce
- 1 small onion, minced
- 1 tsp. ginger

- 1 tsp. salt
- 1/3 cup brown sugar
- 1/3 cup vinegar
- 2 tbs. butter or margarine

Directions:

1. Mix all ingredients in a sauce pan and simmer for half an hour on moderate heat.
2. Stir once in a while.

ULTIMATE SMOKEY SAUCE

Ingredients:

- ¼ cup butter or margarine
- ¼ cup white vinegar
- ¼ tsp. cayenne pepper
- ½ cup catsup
- ½ cup water
- ½ tsp. black pepper
- 1 ½ tsp. liquid smoke
- 1 ½ tsp. salt
- 1 onion, cut in ¼ inch rounds
- 1 tbs. prepared mustard
- 2 tbs. brown sugar
- 2 tbs. lemon juice

- 2 tbs. Worcestershire sauce

Directions:

1. Mix first 10 ingredients in deep cooking pan and mix thoroughly.
2. Bring to its boiling point; then cook, uncovered, on moderate heat for about twenty minutes, stirring once in a while.
3. Mix in rest of the ingredients.
4. Good on chicken, beef or pork.

ULTIMATE TEXAS STYLE SAUCE

Ingredients:

- 1 can (10 ½ ounces) condensed beef broth
- 1 can (6 ½ ounces) tomato paste
- 2 cups chili sauce
- 2 tbs. Worcestershire sauce
- 3 cups dry red wine
- 3 stalks celery
- 4 big onions

Directions:

1. Mix ingredients in a sauce pan and cook on moderate heat for twenty to twenty-five minutes.
2. Stir frequently to keep everything thoroughly combined.

3. When finished, press mixture through a sieve.
4. This makes an excellent marinade for steaks, or just pour it over a beef sandwich.

VERSATILE MUSTARD SAUCE

Goes great with pork, poultry, and sausages.

Ingredients:

- ⅓ cup sugar
- ½ teaspoon salt
- ½ teaspoon Tabasco sauce
- ½ teaspoon white pepper
- 1 cup vinegar, cider or red wine
- 1 cup yellow mustard
- 1 tablespoon Worcestershire sauce
- 1 teaspoon black pepper
- 2 tablespoons butter

Directions:

1. Mix all of the ingredients in a big deep cooking pan. Simmer for half an hour on moderate to low heat.
2. Store in an airtight jar in the refrigerator for maximum 2 weeks.

Yield: 2 cups

VIRGINIA STYLE SAUCE

Ingredients:

- ¼ cup white vinegar
- ¼ tsp. bay leaves, crushed
- ¼ tsp. black pepper
- ½ cup molasses
- ½ tsp. liquid smoke
- ½ tsp. thyme
- 1 can tomato sauce
- 1 tsp. salt

Directions:

1. Mix ingredients in a container until well mixed.
2. Baste frequently.

WEST COAST CHICKEN SAUCE

Ingredients:

- ½ cup catsup
- ½ cup salad oil
- ½ tsp. black pepper
- ½ tsp. chili powder
- 1 clove garlic, grated
- 1 small onion, grated

- 1 tbs. Worcestershire sauce
- 1 tsp. salt
- 2 ½ cups water
- 2 tsp. horseradish
- 2 tsp. sugar

Directions:

1. Mix ingredients in a deep cooking pan and bring to its boiling point.
2. Reduce heat and simmer for five minutes.

WEST COAST SAUCE

Ingredients:

- ¼ cup brown sugar
- ½ tsp. celery salt
- ½ tsp. chili powder
- ½ tsp. dry mustard
- ½ tsp. lemon juice
- 1 12 ounces can tomato puree
- 1 12 ounces can tomato sauce
- 1 clove garlic, minced
- 1 medium onion, chopped fine
- 1 tbs. Worcestershire sauce
- 1 tsp. salt

- 1/8 tsp. pepper
- 1/8 tsp. Tabasco sauce

Directions:

1. Mix the ingredients, in order, in a sauce pan on moderate heat.
2. Bring to its boiling point, then cover and lower heat.
3. Cook for half an hour.

WEST TEXAS SAUCE

Ingredients:

- ½ cup Worcestershire sauce
- ½ tsp. garlic salt
- 1 ½ tsp. Salt
- 1 tsp. black pepper
- 1 tsp. liquid smoke
- 2 cups catsup
- 2 cups strong coffee

Directions:

1. Put ingredients in a deep cooking pan and simmer on moderate heat for half an hour, stirring once in a while.

WHISKEY CREAM SAUCE

Try with smoked salmon, poultry, beef, or wild game.

Ingredients:

- ½ cup whiskey
- ½ teaspoon freshly ground black pepper
- ½ teaspoon sea salt
- 1 bunch green onions
- 1 cup whipping cream
- 2 tablespoons fresh minced Italian parsley
- 2 tablespoons horseradish
- 4 tablespoons butter

Directions:

1. Snip the green part of the onions and save for later.
2. Finely mince the white part of the onions and sauté in butter in a medium-size frying pan until tender.
3. Put in whiskey and cook on moderate heat until reduced to half. Put in cream and horseradish and heat until the mixture coats a spoon.
4. Put in parsley, salt, pepper, and the green part of the onions. Serve instantly.
5. Does not keep well.

Yield: 1¼ cups

WHITE CHICKEN SAUCE

Ingredients:

- ½ cup lemon juice
- ½ cup white vinegar
- 1 cup mayonnaise
- 1 tbs. black pepper
- 1 tbs. salt
- 6 tbs. sugar

Directions:

1. Mix ingredients in container and stir wildly until the desired smoothness is achieved.
2. Baste chicken frequently.

WHITE FISH SAUCE WITH PARSLEY

Time Taken: ten minutes

Ingredients:

- ½ teaspoon ginger powder
- 1 cup mayonnaise
- 1 pinch salt
- 1 tablespoons chopped parsley
- 1 teaspoon white pepper
- 2 tablespoons lime juice

Directions:

1. Mix mayonnaise, lime juice, parsley and ginger powder in a container.
2. Sprinkle with salt and pepper.
3. Serve.

WHITE VINEGAR ROSEMARY SAUCE

Time Taken: 5 minutes

Ingredients:

- ½ cup white vinegar
- 1 tablespoons rosemary, chopped
- 1 teaspoon black pepper
- 1 teaspoon salt
- 2 tablespoons lime juice

Directions:

1. Take a container and put in all ingredients.
2. Mix thoroughly to blend.
3. Barbecue sauce is ready.

WILDFLOWER HONEY VINAIGRETTE

Try this rich sauce with grilled lobster and other shellfish.

Ingredients:

- ¼ cup thoroughly minced mint
- ⅓ cup raspberry vinegar
- ⅓ cup wildflower honey, warmed
- 1 cup olive oil
- 1 tablespoon seasoned pepper
- 1 teaspoon onion salt
- 2 cloves garlic, minced

Directions:

1. Mix all of the ingredients in a wide-mouth glass jar, apart from the olive oil. Cover the jar and shake the ingredients to combine. Take away the lid and slowly whisk in the olive oil.
2. Store placed in the fridge for maximum one week. Will keep longer if the fresh mint is added just before you serve.

Yield: 2 cups

WYOMING BBQ SAUCE

Ingredients:

- ¼ cup white vinegar
- ½ tbs. chili powder
- ½ tbs. salt
- 1 ½ cups melted butter or margarine

- 1 ½ tsp. mustard powder
- 1 ½ tsp. sugar
- 1 big onion, minced
- 1 cup catsup
- 1 tsp. black pepper
- 1 tsp. hot sauce
- 1 tsp. marjoram
- 1 tsp. thyme
- 2 cloves garlic, minced
- 2 tbs. A-1 sauce
- 2 tbs. horseradish
- 6 cups water

Directions:

1. Mix ingredients in a deep cooking pan and cook on moderate to low heat, uncovered,
2. for about forty-five minutes to an hour.

YELLOW SAUCE FOR PORK

Ingredients:

- 1 cup dark brown sugar
- 1 cup prepared mustard
- 1 cup white vinegar

- 1 dash hot sauce
- 1 tsp. black pepper

Directions:

1. Mix ingredients in sauce pan and cook using low heat for about twenty minutes, stirring continuously or until all ingredients are completely blended.
2. Do not boil.
3. Thin slice pork and lay on white bread.
4. Ladle sauce over pork.

YOGURT-MINT SAUCE

Time Taken: ten minutes

Ingredients:

- 1 bunch mint leaves
- 1 cup yogurt
- 1 green chili
- 1 teaspoon salt
- 1-2 garlic cloves
- 2 tablespoons lemon juice

Directions:

1. In a blender put in mint leaves, lemon juice, salt, green chili, garlic and blend well.

2. Move into a container and put in yogurt, mix thoroughly.
3. Serve and enjoy.

ZESTY BEEF OR PORK SAUCE

Ingredients:

- ½ cup brown sugar
- ½ cup butter or margarine
- ½ tsp. dry mustard
- 1 1/3 cup chili sauce
- 1 cup white vinegar
- 1 tbs. onion, minced
- 1 tbs. Worcestershire sauce
- 2 lemons, cut
- 2 tsp. lemon juice

Directions:

1. Mix ingredients in a deep cooking pan and heat until butter melts, stirring continuously.
2. Use high heat.
3. Keep in warm place.

ZESTY CHICKEN SAUCE

Ingredients:

- ¼ cup white vinegar
- 2 tbs. Sugar
- 2 tbs. flour
- 2 tbs. pickle relish
- 1 ½ tbs. lemon juice
- 2 tsp. Worcestershire sauce
- 1 tsp. Salt
- ¼ tsp. hot sauce
- 2/3 cups butter or margarine
- 2/3 cups water

Directions:

1. Melt butter in a deep cooking pan, then put in dry ingredients.
2. Stir until well mixed.
3. Turn off the heat.
4. Gradually mix in rest of the ingredients.
5. Return to heat and cook, stirring continuously until thick and smooth.

ZESTY CHILLI POULTRY BBQ SAUCE

A delicious sauce to baste on grilled chicken and to serve on the side.

Ingredients:

- ¼ cup chili sauce
- ¼ cup lemon juice
- ¼ cup olive oil
- ½ cup water or more to thin sauce, as required
- ½ teaspoon cayenne pepper
- 1 cup ketchup
- 1 red bell pepper, finely chopped
- 1 red onion, finely chopped
- 1 teaspoon chili powder
- 1 teaspoon dry mustard
- 1 teaspoon paprika
- 1 teaspoon salt
- 1 teaspoon seasoned black pepper
- 2 cloves garlic, minced
- 2 tablespoons honey
- 2 tablespoons snipped fresh chives
- 2 tablespoons snipped fresh parsley
- 2 tablespoons steak sauce
- 2 tablespoons Worcestershire sauce

Directions:

1. In a big deep cooking pan, mix all of the ingredients and simmer for about ninety minutes using low heat.
2. Store in an airtight jar in the refrigerator for maximum one week.

Yield: 3½ cups

ZESTY POULTRY SAUCE

Ingredients:

- ¼ cup honey
- ¼ cup prepared mustard
- ½ cup melted butter or margarine
- ½ tsp. black pepper
- ½ tsp. salt
- 1 cup jellied cranberry sauce, mashed
- 2 cloves garlic, mashed
- juice of 1 lemon
- juice of 1 orange

Directions:

1. Mix ingredients in a sauce pan using low heat.
2. Stir until mixed.
3. Brush onto poultry every five minutes.
4. Cook until a golden-brown colour is achieved.

ABOUT THE AUTHOR

Frank Mueller is the owner and pitmaster of Tex Barbecue, based in Austin, Texas. He is a highly regarded pitmaster in U.S, and an author of multiple books on the subject.